trotman

WITHDRAWN

Medicine

UNCOVERED

Careers Uncovered guides aim to expose the truth about what it's really like to work in a particular field, containing unusual and thought-provoking facts about the profession you are interested in. Written in a lively and accessible style, *Careers Uncovered* guides explore the highs and lows of the career, along with the job opportunities and skills and qualities you will need to help you make your way forward.

Titles in this series include:
Accountancy Uncovered
Art and Design Uncovered
Charity and Voluntary Work Uncovered
E-Commerce Uncovered
The Internet Uncovered
Journalism Uncovered, 2nd edition
Law Uncovered, 2nd edition
Marketing and PR Uncovered
Media Uncovered, 2nd edition
Medicine Uncovered, 2nd edition
Music Industry Uncovered, 2nd edition
Nursing and Midwifery Uncovered
Performing Arts Uncovered, 2nd edition
Sport and Fitness Uncovered, 2nd edition
Teaching Uncovered
The Travel Industry Uncovered
Working For Yourself Uncovered

PAUL GREER

Medicine

UNCOVERED

2nd edition

trotman

Medicine Uncovered

This second edition published in 2009 by Trotman Publishing,
a division of Crimson Publishing Ltd., Westminster House,
Kew Road, Richmond, Surrey TW9 2ND

© Trotman Publishing 2009

First edition published in 2003 by Trotman and Company Ltd

Author Paul Greer

British Library Cataloguing in Publication Data
A catalogue record for this book is available from the British Library

ISBN 978 1 84455 174 3

Typeset by RefineCatch Ltd, Bungay, Suffolk

Printed and bound in Great Britain
by Athenaeum Press, Gateshead

CONTENTS

Acknowledgements

The author would like to thank the organisations and individuals who contributed to this book, and in particular Sheila Milner, who was as dependable as ever in producing the typescript.

Paul Greer

CHAPTER 1

What is medicine?

We use the word 'medicine' for a number of things. It can refer to any of the numerous preparations prescribed to ease or cure a condition, to the cluster of professions which are devoted to the reduction of ill-health, or more specifically to the work of doctors or the degree-level training they undertake.

The knowledge and skills practised by general practitioners (GPs) and most hospital staff fall within what is called 'conventional' medicine. This is founded on the largely (though not exclusively) Western developments of the past 400 years or so. The term distinguishes it from 'alternative' (or 'fringe') medicine, which embraces treatments based on beliefs and systems different from the conventional sort. Some of these systems (particularly those of Eastern origin) are thousands of years old, and considered by their practitioners to be in harmony with the human body and mind, in contrast to what they view as the invasive methods of the conventional approach. Many people consult alternative practitioners, and osteopathy and chiropractic are two instances of fringe fields now seen by the public to be virtually part of the medical establishment.

The practice of conventional medicine in Britain is regulated by the General Medical Council (GMC). No one can call him or herself a medical doctor without having successfully completed a long and rigorous university course approved by the GMC, and any doctor found guilty of serious malpractice can be excluded from the profession by removal from its register, a process commonly known as being 'struck off'. This is designed both to promote good practice and encourage public confidence in doctors. Most other jobs in the conventional medical field, from nursing to radiography, have similar safeguards instituted by their governing or professional bodies. The rarity of someone being struck off, despite the demands of the job, is a testimony to the abilities and conscientiousness of the very large majority.

Since medical issues affect many people's lives, they are constantly in the news. Unfortunately, the media often find most appetising the stories which are shocking, or at least unusual, and such coverage should perhaps therefore carry its own health warning. However, TV, radio and newspapers still furnish valuable information on how health services operate and what their main concerns are. The questions which applicants to medical courses are asked at selection interviews suggest that it is well worth following these stories if you're thinking of entering the profession.

Puzzlingly, given the resources it enjoys, medicine sometimes seems to be going backwards rather than forwards. It can sometimes be its own worst enemy: for example, by helping people to live longer medicine enables more of us to reach an age when we are increasingly likely to encounter physical and mental malfunction or breakdown. Also, medical practitioners often advocate health-promoting lifestyles or dietary changes which some patients are reluctant to adopt, even to preserve their own lives. Finally, the time-lag between media-trumpeted successful trials and the availability of a treatment can leave some people feeling they're being denied what others are already getting, which is in fact sometimes the case, owing to varying policies among health services, especially with regard to expensive treatments.

The purpose of this book is to help you see whether medicine might be a career you could enter and enjoy, and it will attempt to do this in the following ways. Chapter 2 leads off with a brief history of the development of medicine up to the present day, and some of the most prominent issues which currently concern it. Chapter 3 describes the personal qualities needed to do the work successfully, some of which you may have already, others of which might be acquired with effort and practice. Chapter 4 explores the entry qualifications and the selection process for medical degree courses – both of which are very rigorous – and what a course at university will involve. It also highlights some of the specialisms open to qualified doctors, usually only after additional training. Chapter 5 features the work of many other jobs in the medical spectrum and includes information on the training and qualifications required for these roles. Chapter 6 covers how you can prepare (for example, by reading, talking to knowledgeable people, and doing work experience) in addition to being aware of the selection tests in use, what might be asked at an interview, and how to create a good impression on your application form – whether for university entry or for your first medical job. Finally, Chapter 7 offers useful sources of information through which to explore further if you wish.

It's important to emphasise that this book is only a starting-point and that if it leaves you thinking seriously about entering the medical profession, you then really need to engage wholeheartedly in the activities it recommends. In particular, competition for places at the 32 medical schools is so keen that would-be applicants must thoroughly test the water, match the personal quality requirements well and be on target for high grades in the right A level subjects.

Sadly, many people who want to become doctors aren't offered the chance to do so. Rather than give up the idea of medical work altogether, however, most could (and many do) opt for an alternative within this general field. Accordingly, this book examines a range of jobs in medicine, one or more of which may turn out for some readers to be as (or even more) attractive than being a doctor. These sections also recognise that many people who'd like to work in a medical capacity don't *want* to become a doctor. In general, medicine is a career which offers good pay, advancement, a stimulating environment, mental and emotional challenges, and at times enormous satisfaction at having helped someone back to health. It's well worth a look!

PORTRAIT: WILLIAM HARVEY (1578–1657)
William Harvey was the first physician in the Western world to describe correctly and in detail the circulatory system of the blood and the properties of the blood as it passed through the system.

FASCINATING FACTS

Coronary bypass surgery was first performed in 1969. It involves attaching blood vessels from the patient's body to the coronary arteries to allow blood to flow freely to the heart, avoiding the atherosclerotic region (the fatty deposits along the inner surface of the arteries).

Fabricius, Harvey's teacher at the University of Padua, had put forward an explanation of the phenomenon, but this did not satisfy his pupil, who in 1616 was able to publish his discovery of the circulatory system in his book (translated from the original Latin as) *An Anatomical Exercise on the Motion of the Heart and Blood in Animals.*

Harvey's explanation, which advanced the concept of a 'closed' system, was at odds with the thinking of his time. However, he had based his conclusions on careful observations made during the vivisections he performed on a range of animals and when tying ligatures on patients. This illustrated the 'one way system' of blood flow, and showed that the theory of the long-revered physician Galen must be in error, since this would require the liver to produce impossibly large quantities of blood. Harvey described a system in which the heart acted as a pump, contrasting with earlier theories which envisaged blood flow as a sucking action of the blood and liver combined.

Harvey lived to the age of 79, long enough to see his ideas accepted during his lifetime. He was personal physician to two monarchs, James I and Charles I, and was able to take advantage of his privileged position to dissect deer from the royal parks. His work did not alter medical practice for some time, though and the practice of blood-letting, for example, still went on. However, he made a significant contribution to medicine, not only by explaining the circulatory system, but by encouraging the scientific method.

CHAPTER 2

A brief history of medicine and some big issues

Possibly the earliest record of medical treatment is the depiction of plants as healing agents in the cave paintings at Lascaux, in France, which date from between 15 000 and 30 000 years ago. However, evidence of more sophisticated practices during the past 5000 years has also emerged. Archaeologists have discovered that at roughly the same time, inhabitants of the Indus Valley, in modern Pakistan, had knowledge of medicine and dentistry; surgery appears to have been performed in Egypt, while empirical observations of disease and illness were carried out in China. Discoveries of Hebrew and Persian medical methods dating from the pre-Christian era have also been made. In all these ancient societies, the concept and practice of medicine dovetailed with belief systems embracing notions of balance and harmony, astral influence, and the will of the gods.

FASCINATING FACTS

Everyone has heard of the Adam's apple and Achilles tendon, but there are nearly 150 other body parts named after people, real or otherwise. The large majority commemorate the doctors or scientists who discovered or investigated them.

In time, however, medical diagnoses and treatments (if still sometimes mistaken) became increasingly based on the human body rather than abstract concepts or religious ideals. The Greek Hippocrates and his followers were the first to describe many medical conditions and to classify illnesses as acute, chronic, endemic, or epidemic. Another Greek, Galen, performed brain and eye surgery, his work being translated into Latin, then the language of European scholarship, in the 1530s.

Drawing on the work of Galen and Hippocrates, Muslim physicians contributed significantly to the development of medicine. Al-Kindi wrote the work *De Gradibus*, demonstrating the value of applying mathematics to medicine, something especially useful in pharmacology, where scales quantifying the strength of drugs were an important development. Another Muslim was Avicenna, whose eleventh-century books *The Canon of Medicine* and *The Book of Healing* were standard works in European and Muslim universities until the seventeenth century. His contributions include identifying the contagious nature of certain diseases, the introduction of quarantine, and the precursor of what we would today call clinical trials. Nevertheless, well into the medieval period, medicine remained a composite of observation and superstition, and, not then being included among the Seven Liberal Arts, was regarded in Europe as a craft rather than a science.

During the Renaissance and Enlightenment periods, however, European medicine in particular became characterised by experimental investigation, for example by means of dissection. Through men like Andreas Vesalius and William Harvey (who first described the circulation of the blood) understanding and diagnosis improved, but the absence of effective drugs still proved a major obstacle to widespread better health and, as late as the 1840s, Ignaz Semmelweis dramatically reduced the death rate among new mothers by requiring doctors to wash their hands before attending

women in childbirth. Through the work of Edward Jenner a
smallpox vaccine was developed, while in the 1860s Joseph Lister
established the principles of antisepsis. About the same time,
Gregor Mendel framed the laws which became the basis of modern
genetics and, in 1885, Louis Pasteur produced a vaccine against
rabies and (with Claude Bernard) developed the process of
pasteurisation used in food production today. The nineteenth
century also saw women begin to play a recognised role, with
Florence Nightingale establishing a hospital for soldiers in the
Crimea, rapidly lowering patient mortality mainly through good
hygiene and proper nutrition. However, full recognition and
application of some developments during this period were
delayed because of conservatism in medical circles.

FASCINATING FACTS

In 1724, Daniel Gabriel Fahrenheit, who manufactured
thermometers, produced a temperature scale very similar to
the one which now bears his name. Later advances were made
by Anders Celsius and by Sir Thomas Allbutt, who invented a
clinical thermometer which produced a body temperature
reading in five minutes, much faster than the previous average
of 20.

Great and speedy strides were taken in the twentieth century with
the discovery of sulphanilamide (the first antibiotic), widespread
vaccination programmes, chemotherapy in the treatment of cancer,
and the discovery of the structure of DNA, which formed the basis
for the next leap in genetics. Technical innovations, too, played a
big part, through inventions such as Roentgen's X-rays, the
electrocardiograph for monitoring the body, and the mass
production of the antibiotic penicillin. Transplant surgery was
headline news in the second half of the 1960s when the South
African heart specialist Dr Christiaan Barnard was accorded
celebrity status following the first successful human heart
transplant. There were developments in the treatment of mental
illness, too. Emil Kraepelin introduced new medical categories for
known disorders, and in the 1950s new psychiatric drugs appeared.
In the course of the past 20 years or so, the advent of information
technology has facilitated the communication of ideas, and data

collection and analysis made large-scale research programmes and the comparison of results much easier, leading to more reliable conclusions and, ultimately, solutions.

Inspiring as the work of pioneers may be, successful healthcare provision for large populations depends on sound principles and good organisation. In 1937, the author A J Cronin (who was also a doctor) published a novel called *The Citadel*, in which many serious questions were posed about the inadequacies of healthcare in Britain, including the inability of many people to pay for treatment. The 1942 report of the economist and social reformer William Beveridge led to Clement Attlee's Labour Government conceiving of the 'cradle to grave' free healthcare which was introduced for practical purposes in 1948 and has been enjoyed ever since (currently by about 92 per cent of the population). This is, of course, the National Health Service (NHS), which is governed by the Department of Health, but controlled by 10 Strategic Health Authorities overseeing the work of about 150 Primary Care Trusts (PCT), which use the services of about 30 000 doctors and 18 000 dentists. The NHS has an annual budget of just over £100 billion, the cost being met largely through National Insurance contributions from employers, employees and self-employed people. All services are free, except for most adult prescriptions, optical services and dental services (where most charges are still much lower than for private work). At the time of writing, a target waiting period of no longer than 18 weeks for any treatment has been set for the end of 2008.

FASCINATING FACTS

The NHS is the largest employer in Europe, with 1.3 million staff, and treats over 3 million people every *week*. Its annual budget is over £100 *billion*.

The following six medical issues are among those most often in the news.

SAFETY

The safety of both patients and staff, especially in hospitals, has presented a number of problems, particularly in recent years.

Cleanliness is one of these and there have been a number of media horror stories about patients being additionally vulnerable on account of poor standards of hygiene on wards. It has been suggested that in some institutions this is because budgetary cuts have left less money to pay for cleaning, or that the work has been sub-contracted to organisations whose workers are themselves under pressure, or who don't understand the level of cleanliness required. In some hospitals, procedures which constitute what has become known as 'deep cleaning' are undertaken to minimise risks to health.

Hospitals have traditionally been places with very open access. Large numbers of friends and relatives come to visit patients and they can't all be kept under surveillance. However, isolated but very unpleasant attacks on staff and patients have raised the security profile, and medical workers are expected to wear identification badges at all times. They must also be ready to challenge anyone they feel is up to no good, and if necessary to call security staff, who are now more visible.

The right of medical staff to work safely is also increasingly recognised, with less expectation that they should have to calm or restrain aggressive or violent patients. Nevertheless, certain departments, such as accident and emergency, are likely to receive more than their share of drunk or abusive visitors, so, while not expected to handle every situation, front-line staff are now trained to avoid or defuse confrontations.

Anyone concerned by these things should bear in mind that safety issues are taken very seriously throughout the medical profession and that the large majority of patients and visitors are well behaved, grateful for the work staff do, and respectful of them.

THE AGEING POPULATION

In the United Kingdom (and Europe as a whole), an increasing proportion of the population is over the age of 65. In addition, more are living into their 80 and 90s, with about 9000 people resident in Britain having passed their 100th birthday. These are significant facts for the medical professions and pose big questions for them about the quantity and nature of resources to be devoted to those in older age groups. This already considerable task has not been made easier by recent legislation which discourages or prohibits policies or actions dismissive of the needs and wishes of older people.

Medicine is often a victim of its own success, as ever-improving methods of care and treatment extend the lives of people who later on need more care and treatment, placing increased strain on often already-stretched services. In fact, the greatest single input of medical resources in a person's life is typically during the last month of it. Also, because families are increasingly fragmented, more elderly people live alone and depend on equipment to aid their mobility, as well as visits from carers and practitioners. Because relatives may not be available as intermediaries, doctors and others must take particular care to ensure that older people understand what treatment they may need, or how to take any medication prescribed.

FASCINATING FACTS

There are currently about 9000 centenarians in Britain. At the time of writing, the oldest British man has just celebrated his 112th birthday. He is one of only three surviving British veterans of the First World War.

One of the big medical successes of recent years has been joint replacement, which, though major surgery, is comparatively straightforward, and enjoys a high success rate. In addition to the resources needed for the operation, rehabilitative work, such as physiotherapy to attain full mobility, is required. While such undertakings are unquestionably of enormous benefit to individuals, they are most common among the older age groups and still have to be paid for.

OBESITY

Figures vary, but there is strong evidence that many people in countries around the world are unhealthily overweight. In 2004, a report entitled *Storing Up Problems* was published by the Royal

College of Physicians, the Faculty of Public Health, and the Royal College of Paediatrics and Child Health. It was followed by a House of Commons Select Committee report on the impact of obesity on health and society in the UK and possible ways to address the problems it presented. In 2006, the National Institute for Health and Clinical Excellence (NICE) issued a guideline on the diagnosis and management of obesity and the policy implications of this for non-healthcare organisations, especially within local communities. A 2007 report produced by Sir Derek Wanless for the King's Fund sounded the warning that, without further action, obesity could financially cripple the NHS.

Obesity is a condition in which the body's natural energy reserve, stored in fatty tissue, exceeds healthy limits. It is calculated on a scale known as the Body Mass Index (or BMI), conceived by the Belgian statistician Adolphe Quetelet, and is in essence a weight/height ratio. World Health Organisation (WHO) figures published in 2000 set the healthy range of BMI from 18.5–25, the overweight range at 25–30, and 30–40 as obese, with 40+ as severely or morbidly obese. Body fat can also be assessed by measuring precisely a pinch of skin to calculate the subcutaneous fat layer. BMI is not taken as the sole predictor of unhealthy conditions, and doctors also take into account factors such as race, ethnicity, musculature, age, and sex when interpreting its significance for an individual.

A number of serious and life-threatening medical conditions have been linked with obesity, including diabetes, cancer, cardiovascular disease, liver disease, stroke, respiratory difficulties, and depression. The incidence of obesity has increased in the past 50 years, but in the past 20 particularly. There is no simple explanation for this, but a number of factors are considered to be contributory:

- a reduction in home-cooking and an increase in the consumption of high-calorie fast food

- the use of computers at work resulting in more jobs being sedentary

- fewer children walking to school or social events, most travelling by car instead

- messages about healthy eating and exercise being ignored

- less time spent by schoolchildren doing PE

- the likelihood that children of overweight couples will grow up to be overweight themselves

- a mistaken belief in medical intervention as a last resort

- some people claiming the right to be fat.

In extreme cases, surgery may be an option, but less radical methods are preferable for most people. These range from educating individuals about the causes of obesity, offering healthier school dinners, increasing sport and fitness facilities and encouraging people to walk or cycle to work or school. It has also been suggested that expensive treatment should be denied in cases where obesity is the cause of the medical condition. However, this is considered an extreme view by most people.

Obesity is undoubtedly an issue where prevention is better than cure, yet the former depends on so much more than medical services – government initiatives, local authority regulation, community spirit and individual will-power to name only four. The picture is further complicated when we think of how many people are struggling with the problem in our busy modern society. They fail to help themselves, but for understandable reasons: cooking fast food because they're tired after work; running parental 'taxi services' for children because of safety concerns; or comfort eating after giving up smoking. These are among the things which, quite apart from medical knowledge, a practitioner has to understand and deal with to begin to help a patient who is obese.

AVAILABILITY OF TREATMENT

While there can be no doubt that the large majority of those who work in health-related occupations are committed primarily to the well-being of patients, this obscures the effect of other forces. The profit motive is one of these, and very much related to the business decisions of, for example, drug companies. These organisations devote many millions of pounds to research and development and can't afford to spend such resources turning out unsalable products. Very expensive medications may be worth their price-tag because they offer much-needed relief from serious conditions, but if the cost makes only limited supplies available, not everyone will benefit.

With the exception of private patients, who receives certain treatments is usually the decision of the local authority which foots the bill. This can lead to situations where a person in one town gets the treatment they need, while someone in a neighbouring one is denied it, and it's not unknown for people to move area to become eligible for treatment. There is ongoing debate as to whether this should be necessary, or even possible, since someone relocating for this purpose immediately becomes a drain on the new authority's resources. Whether certain newcomer groups, such as immigrants or asylum seekers, should have immediate free access to health services is also increasingly discussed.

Though government targets as well as concern for people's well-being have significantly reduced NHS waiting-times generally, those who can afford it often choose to be treated privately, resulting in speedier treatment and recovery in (often) more agreeable surroundings. It's sometimes argued that doctors (mostly trained at the state's expense) should not be free to earn the handsome fees which go with this work, but the result of restricting their choices might simply cause some to decamp to the private sector and be lost altogether to the NHS. It may also be argued that this freedom keeps good doctors motivated and that new and more sophisticated forms of treatment and care available in the private sector are in time adopted in NHS institutions.

ORGAN DONATION

When someone dies, their body may still prove useful if one or more of their organs is transplanted into a patient whose body is failing. Kidney, lung, pancreas and liver transplants are relatively commonplace, and even heart transplants are now over 40 years old. Currently, no one's organs are used at their death without permission and many people in good health carry organ donor cards to enable medical staff to remove organs without delay at their death. In Britain, there is an Organ Donations Register to which all NHS hospitals have access. Organs are always urgently needed and, where there is no advance consent available, newly-bereaved relatives may be asked whether they would consider donating their loved one's organs. This is among the least enviable tasks a doctor will have to perform and one requiring enormous tact and sensitivity. However, because most people who die in hospital have an infection of some kind, only a small proportion are potential donors.

At the time of writing, there is controversy over a government proposal to reverse the situation relating to consent, making someone's organs fair game once they are dead unless a wish to the contrary has been expressed beforehand. This is sometimes known as the 'dissent solution' and is appealing because in those countries where it has been adopted there is (with the exception of kidneys) no longer an organ waiting list of would-be recipients.

Moral considerations related to such issues fall under the umbrella term 'bioethics' and, in the past 30 years or so, bioethics have become increasingly prominent because what medical techniques can achieve raises questions about what it's right to do in particular circumstances. One such question in relation to organ donation concerns when someone can be considered dead. This is commonly agreed to be when there is no detectable brain-stem activity, but so rigorous a definition renders many organs unsuitable for donation, and in some countries a more relaxed one has been adopted to aid potential recipients.

'Transplant tourism' is also an issue. This occurs when organs are obtained through unofficial sources (often from needy people in third-world countries) via less-than-reputable agents to whom well-heeled recipients pay large amounts of money. In addition to the dubious environments within which the operations to obtain organs are done, it is believed that many donors are exploited, either because the medical risks or emergencies aren't explained to them, or because they don't receive their promised money. Those who defend the procedure say that it is better that some people are exploited than that others die, but it may be that a significant proportion of donors die as well as being exploited, whether or not their organs save other people.

Other issues aired in connection with organ donation include whether people in certain categories should be permitted to receive them. For instance, should convicted prisoners be eligible? Or, more specifically, should an alcoholic receive a healthy liver transplant which might be ruined by further drinking instead of helping someone else? There is concern in some quarters over whether cloning should be engaged in, if the object is only to produce a ready source of organs. Even xenotransplantation (the use of animal organs for humans) is questioned, particularly by some animal rights groups, who hold that an animal should not be sacrificed to assist a human, which they would consider reflects a prejudice often called 'speciesism'.

Great improvements in medical techniques now mean that a transplanted organ is much less likely to be rejected by its new host, so living donors can have the satisfaction of knowing their gift is likely to be of maximum benefit. Technology has also helped, with the internet facilitating the hunt for good Samaritan donors.

FASCINATING FACTS

The human body has over 20 internal organs, some of which are exclusively male or female. They are the adrenals, appendix, bladder, brain, eyes, gall bladder, heart, intestines, kidney, liver, lungs, oesophagus, ovaries, pancreas, parathyroids, pituitary, prostate, spleen, stomach, testicles, thymus, thyroid, uterus and veins.

PAY AND WORKING HOURS

Traditionally there has been considerable variation among the earnings of those working in the medical field, with doctors and dentists occupying the top spots on the table and nurses at or near the bottom. Their relative positions are probably the same today, but nurses are certainly better off than they were a few years ago and many doctors are at the higher end of the salary scale in most communities. However, the value which these higher earnings reflects does not render staff the less vulnerable in the event of financial strictures, and redundancies among even urgently needed nurses have sometimes been made by services strapped for cash.

However, qualified medical workers who are prepared to move still enjoy a strong position, with vacancies elsewhere in the NHS, the private sector, and even abroad, where British qualifications are highly respected.

Another quality strongly associated with medical professionals (and doctors in particular) is commitment. Because their services are so vital and because they enjoy respect and good pay, they have been expected to work very long hours with little recognition of how this adversely affects their efficiency. However, in recent years, hospital doctors' official and real hours have been reduced, and this trend is even more marked among GPs, with people being encouraged to drop in to medical centres, thus allowing doctors to use their time more effectively. Technology has helped, too: patients unable to keep appointments can leave messages more easily; and databases allow more efficient record-keeping and booking systems.

Nevertheless, there is still a perception of nurses being underpaid, and there was a recent appeal to professional footballers to donate a day's salary to the cause of nurses' pay. However, pay-scales for most medical jobs have fairly high senior rates, meaning that while initial earnings are sometimes modest, prospects are good, and even nurses can earn well over the national average salary, particularly if they attain the status of nurse consultant.

FASCINATING FACTS

A vaccine for the disease polio was discovered during the 1950s. A few decades earlier, one of its victims had been Franklin D Roosevelt, who, later, as President of the United States, conducted his three terms of office from a wheelchair.

PORTRAIT: EDWARD JENNER (1749–1823)

In the middle of the eighteenth century, when Jenner was born, the mortality rate for variola major, the severe form of smallpox, was still very high. However, there was an informal belief among farming communities that contracting the relatively mild cowpox resulted in immunity against the more serious disease. The story goes that a milkmaid suffering from cowpox came to Jenner, a doctor in the Gloucestershire town of Berkeley, for treatment. He had long suspected the link between cowpox and smallpox, and took the opportunity to inject the eight-year old son of his gardener with a mild dose of the former. He later injected him with smallpox, to which he proved immune. Jenner perfected a vaccine in 1796, and by 1800 his findings had been published throughout Europe and the United States. The practice of vaccination continued in Britain until 1974 and five years after that the World Health Organisation declared smallpox officially eradicated worldwide.

Have you

2 years?
Ever been, or are
Received a Dis...
Suffered from
Had a chest
place / date

CHAPTER 3

Personal qualities needed

This chapter covers the qualities necessary or useful for work in the field of medicine. While all those featured are particularly valuable for a doctor, most are also relevant to other medical jobs.

GOOD COMMUNICATION SKILLS

Good communication skills are vital in medical work – literally vital, as lives can often depend on them. There are several main ways in which doctors and others must communicate successfully:

- they need to establish quickly a good rapport with their patients, to draw out of them the information needed to make a diagnosis and decide on treatment

- they need to explain to patients what's wrong with them, what treatment is to be given, and the patient's part in a full and speedy recovery and

- they need to explain to family members what will be required at home, possibly including frequency and dosage of medication.

In these sorts of exchanges, it's important to command respect without being intimidating, and training includes the establishment of a good 'bedside manner' with which both practitioner and patient are comfortable. Medical professionals also have to communicate effectively with colleagues, which may include those in other specialisms. They must therefore be respectful of others' expertise, yet able to express their own (possibly differing) view with confidence. A doctor who can listen to others before making decisions is likely to be rewarded with patients who make better progress. Medical professionals must also keep meticulous records of those they treat, and these must be quickly intelligible to their colleagues. Computer databases help, but there are still times when (contrary to the popular image) doctors have to write clearly! Finally, most medical information on individuals is confidential, so practitioners must take care not to breach the rules relating to this.

ATTENTION TO DETAIL

Attention to detail is essential, and good observation is a part of this, since even a slight alteration in a patient's appearance may herald a change in their condition. This may come easier to GPs who are likely to see the same patients more often than their hospital counterparts. Visual evidence is only part of the doctor's armoury though, and he or she must be able to draw important conclusions from indicators such as temperature and blood pressure readings. However, detail is important not only in diagnosis or tracking progress, but in treatment, too. A good practitioner will enquire about patients' circumstances, and their domestic situations in particular, to avoid any treatment being undermined by the demands of their lives. This may even extend to their home or work environments, since discomfort may be eliminated or reduced by introducing facilities there, perhaps with the help of an occupational therapist.

STAMINA

Stamina is one of the most important attributes of doctors and other medical workers because many of them work long hours to begin with, and may have to extend these in emergencies. GPs do a lot of their work sitting down, but many hospital staff are on their feet most of the day. Moreover, the work is mentally as well as physically taxing, and you can't just engage low gear when you're tired, since high standards must be maintained at all times lest patients be put at risk. No one's energy is limitless, so you must learn the most economical ways of doing things, and not neglect opportunities for relaxation. Also, you cannot afford to become emotionally involved in patients' situations, as you're likely to become distressed when they can't be helped or if they die. Fortunately, the strains of the job are often counterbalanced by its variety and the satisfaction which comes from doing it well.

DEXTERITY

As a medical practitioner, you have to be dextrous. This may be in setting up and operating equipment, performing minor operations, manipulating a joint, setting a broken bone, stitching a wound, giving an injection, measuring out liquids, and bandaging, to name a few. Sometimes you need to be dextrous to work in unison with a colleague, or when attempting a procedure where you are inhibited by the patient's pain or limited movement. In such situations, you must work speedily and economically without being any the less effective. Dexterity is also important in earning patients' trust. They're more likely to respect you if they see you performing tasks confidently and competently. Exceptional manual dexterity is a quality useful for would-be surgeons, though technology, which includes miniature cameras, now allows the surgeon to undertake even the trickiest operations more easily.

GOOD ORGANISATIONAL SKILLS

All medical practitioners have to fit a lot into their working day, so must be well organised. They have to know who their patients are, and be conversant with each one's particular condition and current state. They must know what facilities or equipment they'll require, and ensure these are available. They need an awareness of time and to be able to use it effectively, not spending so long with some patients that others are neglected. They need to ensure their records are kept up to date, and know when best to contact colleagues or organisations, and keep others informed of their movements so that they can be reached quickly when necessary.

To take full advantage of meetings with colleagues, they may need to prepare for agenda items. Medical services must be available to the public at all times, so advance planning is essential to ensure cover during holidays or when colleagues are absent for any reason. Medical practitioners therefore also have to ensure that people close to them understand how committed they must be, to avoid friction in their personal lives.

SELF-ASSURANCE (WITH HUMILITY)

Many medical practitioners work alone much of the time, and therefore largely free of reliance on others. Some jobs are very specialised, and even in a hospital a small team only may be responsible for all the work in a particular field, and each member of it be a real expert rarely requiring help. However, where a wide range of very differing conditions and problems are encountered (as, say, by GPs), you need to recognise where your own knowledge or skill may be insufficient, and be willing to consult with a colleague or refer your patient to an appropriate specialist. This can easily be done where good hospital facilities are within easy reach; however, in rural areas a doctor may want to spare a patient the trouble or physical difficulty of a long trip. The inconvenience the patient escapes by being treated by the GP is only of value if the case is within the doctor's competence. No responsible doctor will stretch the bounds of his or her expertise where this places a patient at risk, and all medical practitioners must have a sense of their own limits to be sure this does not happen.

EXHIBITING AND ENCOURAGING CONFIDENCE

All medical professionals from time to time encounter situations which leave them scratching their heads, but this is no reason for them to lose confidence in themselves, nor their colleagues or patients in them. Behaving confidently even when faced with a difficult challenge is positive and professional; it helps to inject assurance, and reassure others involved. Nor does it mean being dishonest. The admission of a difficulty is probably best accompanied by an explanation of how it's come about and possible ways to resolve it, though technical terms should be avoided where these are inappropriate. However, a good explanation of a situation in layman's language to your patient as you work through the problem may actually raise their trust, impressing them with your truthful manner.

COMMITMENT

Commitment is an attitude, but one which translates meaningfully into actions. Many of these are everyday things, such as being punctual; having case notes or other relevant information to hand; and providing explanations to patients to reduce their anxiety, better understand their condition, and enable them to make their own contribution to their recovery. You should also keep up to date with medical information and techniques through reading, trying to learn from more experienced colleagues, and even being willing to make a challenging career move to become a better practitioner.

It also means taking care of yourself, so that you can accomplish your work most effectively. Sadly, doctors have not always been the best adverts for healthy living, the pressures of the job leading many to smoke, drink, or obtain less sleep than they need. However, this now seems less prevalent, and perhaps healthier-looking doctors are more likely to have patients follow their advice. Commitment comes from feeling you can make a difference, and as a practitioner you should remind yourself of your own good work and successes, as there will be occasions when a patient's death or failure to improve are likely to prove discouraging.

AN ENQUIRING SPIRIT

Most would-be medical professionals begin their training with an enquiring spirit, and some retain it all their working lives. However, this outlook is sometimes difficult to sustain in the face of prolonged demanding work, and perhaps harder still when your knowledge seems to have plateaued and few goals appear on the horizon. For those with the interest and determination, though, medicine is a field which offers more stimulation than most, as the human condition, both physical and psychological, is always throwing up something new worth understanding. This may come in the course of dealing with patients, but an experienced practitioner with a methodical scientific bent may find this appetite better satisfied through research. While it's not impossible for an individual to do this, projects which produce reliable findings are more likely to be gained through hospitals or centre-based teams focusing on a particular phenomenon or practice. Published research in science and medical journals and books can lead the more prominent investigators into running lectures and seminars at conferences, and to enjoy the kudos which accompanies being a recognised expert or authority.

ADAPTABILITY

Much of the time, doctors and other practitioners work within well-established systems, either in their own practice, a clinic, or hospital department. These systems will have been devised and tailored to allow the maximum number of patients to be seen efficiently and effectively. In special circumstances, however, doctors and others must be ready to bend rules or break habits in the interests of the patient – for example, by doing a home visit rather than expect them to visit the surgery, or to cover for an absent colleague. People don't conveniently stop being ill or having accidents at Christmas or on weekends, and there will be occasions when you must sacrifice your well-earned time off to ensure the well-being of a patient. Adaptability (not to say ingenuity) may be required at times if necessary equipment is unavailable or malfunctions, or even (in an emergency) the help of a lay person has to be enlisted in place of a fellow professional.

MATURITY

Because their training is long, doctors typically are not qualified until well into their 20s, and this is only a little less true of others in the medical field whose work requires a degree or postgraduate qualification. This has advantages, since being an effective practitioner depends not only on grasping a large body of difficult knowledge and having the skill to use it, but being able to make informed decisions under pressure, possessing a common-sense order of priorities, and being able to adopt a manner appropriate to each patient in the circumstances. You also need to understand why some patients behave in ways unlikely to aid their cure or rehabilitation, as this may help you to encourage them more effectively. Many practitioners with considerable experience still are (and look) young, and may not get the respect they deserve from some patients. It's therefore in your interests to convey maturity, for example through an assured way of speaking and firm decision-making, without losing the personal touch. Such a manner should help you gain your colleagues' respect, especially where your approach to a patient or a problem differs from their own. It's obvious from all this that working in medicine makes you grow up very quickly!

PERSONAL RESPONSIBILITY AND WILLINGNESS TO DELEGATE

As a medical practitioner you need a strong sense of personal responsibility, ensuring you do all you can to achieve the comfort and well-being of the patients in your care. However, as your responsibilities increase in the course of your career, you must draw a line between what you *can* do and what you should leave to others. This is particularly important in hospital work, where there may be several levels of seniority. Some responsibilities will come automatically as part of a designated role, but you may at times have to choose where you allocate duties. This is where being a good judge of junior colleagues' capacities comes in (another element in the maturity mentioned earlier), and is important not just to avoid exhausting yourself, but to help colleagues gain wider knowledge and grow in confidence. This is essential in medical work, where tasks are often carried out by teams rather than individuals, and the danger of a unit or department becoming dependent on any particular person (at any level) is reduced by taking pains to entrust things to others. Of course, the business of delegating itself becomes a serious responsibility, as the professional wisdom or otherwise with which this is accomplished becomes more apparent the larger the scale on which it's done.

TOLERANCE AND TACT

Tolerance should not be interpreted as putting up with things that should be remedied. Rather it means recognising, as a practitioner, limitations (in yourself, others, or systems) which reduce effectiveness but are unavoidable. These may range from government health funding, to hospital senior management, or to patients conducting themselves in ways not conducive to their recovery. Tact can be a strong weapon in your armoury in combating some of these trials: it may not be possible to berate the Minister of Health personally, but a diplomatic approach with colleagues and patients may improve some daily shortcomings. As a practitioner, you must be tolerant with yourself too, for example when a patient does not improve or dies, despite your best efforts. Also, medical practitioners, like everyone else, make mistakes. Fortunately, most do not have serious consequences and can be learned from.

HUMOUR

A sense of humour is a very important attribute for people working in medicine. It acts as a safety valve to prevent the suffering of patients and the predicament of their loved ones getting you down. It's more about having a certain lightness in outlook or attitude rather than telling funny stories; responding to what happens rather than creating humorous situations. A sense of humour which can be incorporated into dealings with patients can be helpful in bringing a sense of proportion to people who may be understandably down about what's happening to them. However, as well as being appropriate to the situation, humour must be a reflection of your own personality, as it will seem empty if only assumed for form's sake.

ABILITY TO KEEP THINGS IN PERSPECTIVE

Humour is only one of the tools you can use to help keep things in perspective. Colleagues, especially more experienced ones, can be invaluable, too, as they will have had to come to terms with the concerns that may be troubling you. From time to time it may be worth making a mental list of what you've achieved, to set against what you haven't, or to remind yourself of the advances in medicine over the years which have permitted control or cure of conditions which were once killers. As a doctor or other medical professional, it's not wrong to have feelings about what you see and experience through your work, but controlling their impact is in itself part of the job.

FASCINATING FACT

Florence Nightingale was named after the city where she was born.

PORTRAIT: FLORENCE NIGHTINGALE (1820–1910)

Born into a rich, upper-class family, Florence Nightingale defied their wishes from an early age by committing herself to becoming a nurse. She became a leading advocate for improved medical care in infirmaries, and took a post as superintendent of the Institute for the Care of Sick Gentlemen, in London, in 1853. When, the following year, reports of dreadful conditions in the war in the Crimea, in Turkey, reached England, she led a small group of women volunteer nurses there. They found the barracks at Scutari accommodating wounded soldiers in overcrowded conditions and cared for by overworked staff. Hygiene was almost non-existent, there was little in the way of medicine, and infection was rife, with cholera, dysentery and typhoid unchecked. This, along with a lack of nutritious food, had created a dreadful state of affairs to which the powers-that-be seemed indifferent. Successfully marshalling her force of nurses, and making the most of her exalted family connections, Florence Nightingale effected changes so dramatic that only six months after her arrival, death rates had sharply reduced. Her later report to the Royal Commission on the Health of the Army helped to reduce fatalities in peacetime as well as in war, partly through the establishment of an Army Medical School and a comprehensive record system. In 1855, the Nightingale Fund for the Training of Nurses was established, and five years later the Nightingale Training School was set up at St Thomas's Hospital. Her book *Notes on Nursing* became both a standard medical text and a bestseller with the public. By the 1880s Nightingale nurses were increasingly influential in the growing nursing profession, several of them becoming matrons at hospitals in Britain and abroad. Florence Nightingale was awarded the Order of Merit in 1907, three years before her death at the age of 90. International Nurses Day is still celebrated on her birthday.

CHAPTER 4

Training to be a doctor

BECOMING A DOCTOR

Anyone wanting to become a doctor must be accepted for training by a department of medicine at a university, also known as 'medical school'. People trying for medical school often consider A levels the first hurdle. In fact, it should be GCSEs, since these grades offer university selectors the first independent measure of your academic ability and potential. While a string of B or C grades may be enough for most study purposes post-16, they are unlikely to impress medical schools, who will expect to see a generous sprinkling of A and A* grades, particularly in sciences, which should, if possible, be offered as individual subjects (chemistry, biology etc) rather than in combined form. No fewer than eight GCSE subject passes should be offered, to include English Language and Maths at grade B minimum. It is no exaggeration to say that every year there are many applicants (perhaps even a majority) who far exceed these requirements.

There are 32 medical schools at British universities, and you're unlikely to be offered a place on a degree course in medicine without actual or expected A level grades of at least ABB. One of these should be chemistry and another biology (though some schools will accept biology at AS level, too, at grade B minimum).

However, these alone won't guarantee a place. Selectors also look for signs of a deep interest in medicine, commitment to it as a career, and the personal qualities likely to shape a good doctor. Some medical schools admit a small number of applicants with excellent grades in non-science A levels, but they must undertake a preparatory year to acquire the necessary grounding in science. Students offering the International Baccalaureate can also apply. You will need about 36 points and your science still needs to be very strong.

FASCINATING FACTS

About 30 per cent of the annual intake of British medical schools are from ethnic minorities, and about 60 per cent of the total are women.

Medical degree courses normally last five (occasionally six) years, and the academic year is longer than the traditional university one, lasting 40 or more weeks rather than the usual 30. You therefore need real commitment and stamina to sustain focus and intensity for so long. Much of the course is necessarily academic, but students now are introduced early on to settings in which they meet patients and can learn from direct observation and questioning. There are strong common elements among medical degree courses, but some important differences, too, such as in terms of emphasis or the optional units offered. You can apply to a maximum of four medical schools, and should possess a good knowledge of each one, along with the university of which it is part. Some courses teach largely through problem-based learning, while some are more traditionally exam-oriented than others.

The GMC report *Tomorrow's Doctors* encouraged medical schools to reduce the amount of factual knowledge students were expected to imbibe during their first two years, leaving time to develop those skills and attitudes most important in the job itself. The schools were also encouraged to offer special study modules to allow students an early focus on projects of particular interest to them. Problem-based learning was also introduced, whereby factual material is taught within the presentation of real-life cases. The main purpose has been to place less emphasis on turning out doctors as 'finished products', but rather ones capable of learning and adapting in the course of their careers as medicine itself continues to change and develop.

The introduction of clinical skills laboratories enables students to learn and practise procedures on dummies, building confidence partly through repetition, something which reduces the risk of error with real patients on the wards. These wards are in local teaching hospitals and district general hospitals. Students' stays there are known as 'attachments', and free accommodation is normally provided if the hospital is too far for an easy daily return trip. The increase in trainee doctors in recent years has meant many students spending longer periods further away than in the past, reducing the communal feeling which comes with learning as a group. If you find yourself on such a placement, it's important to keep in contact with fellow students (by phone, email or text) if you don't see one another for a while, to avoid feeling isolated.

The intensity and length of the typical day means that medical students tend to socialise among themselves rather than with people from other departments. However, there is still usually a good social mix, as year groups often number 200 or more, are constituted of people from both state and private education, and many of whom excel at more than just exams. The fact that the course exposes students to many maturing experiences also draws people together.

Some medical courses offer students the option of putting things on hold for one or two years to study for what is called an 'intercalated' degree. This is a medical science qualification especially useful for anyone considering a career in research. Fees will probably be paid, but you may still have to finance normal living expenses. Most courses also offer the chance to spend two or three months on a period of self-directed learning, known as an 'elective'. This may be undertaken in Britain, but often provides an excellent opportunity to see how medicine is practised abroad, or to examine a medical issue especially prominent in a particular country. Grants and prizes are available to help fund electives, so you can probably afford to be ambitious and imaginative. Special study modules may be available, and some medical schools offer exchanges in other European countries via the Erasmus programme.

FURTHER TRAINING

THE FOUNDATION PROGRAMME

On successfully completing their degree courses in medicine, doctors embark on the Foundation Programme. This lasts two years and replaces what were known as the pre-registration house officer year and the first year of senior house officer training. During this period, they are called 'foundation doctors', or, more precisely, as 'foundation house officer 1' in the first year, and 'foundation house officer 2' in the second. Those on the programme are trained and assessed against competencies approved by the GMC.

New doctors obtain their places on the Foundation Programme through a national application process, and in competition with other medical graduates. Training is offered in a range of settings, embracing community, acute, mental health and general practice work. Foundation Year 1 includes three months in a surgical post and three in a medical one. Work-based assessments are made regularly, and trainees maintain a national learning portfolio. On completing Year 1, doctors progress automatically to Year 2, which consists of three varied four-month placements. At least one of these is in a shortage speciality, and doctors can try out additional specialisms before committing to one. As in Year 1, regular work-based assessments are made. On completing the two-year Foundation Programme, all doctors will, whatever their placements, have achieved the same clinical and non-clinical competencies. Further information on the programme is available at www.foundationprogramme.nhs.uk.

RUN-THROUGH AND SPECIALIST TRAINING

Run-through and specialist training is part of the new career framework for doctors introduced in 2007. While on the Foundation Programme, a doctor can apply for run-through specialist training to begin immediately after it. This lasts several years, on average three for intending GPs and five to seven for other specialisms. Successful completion leads to the Certificate of Completion of Specialist Training (CCST).

Instead of starting run-through specialist training straight after their Foundation Programme, doctors may apply for a fixed-term training post. These are offered in hospitals alone, normally last only a year, and must be applied for individually. They are proper training posts, but no developmental programmes are offered beyond the second such year. While so occupied, a doctor is free to apply for GP or other specialist training, or for a fixed-term post in another speciality.

Another career option at this stage is as a medical academic, but this usually requires a research degree on top of the medical one. Further information on run-through and other specialist training routes can be found at the Modernising Medical Career website: www.mmc.nhs.uk.

THE WORK

Most qualified doctors work as GPs or in hospitals. Here is some information about work in each sector.

GENERAL PRACTITIONER

Most GPs are employed by PCTs. These may include a number of GP surgeries, plus clinics or similar establishments within which other health professionals such as dentists, opticians or physiotherapists may work. Time spent with patients may be in the surgery or clinic, or in the patient's home (though home visits are now becoming less common). Surgery hours are set by the doctors themselves, and usually include early evening and some weekend opening. At the time of writing, there are discussions in government circles over whether to extend the number of hours to which GPs are available to patients. Most patient contacts are spent checking for the occurrence or on the progress of a condition; making assessments using procedures such as blood tests or X-rays; writing prescriptions and offering instructions on medication; issuing certificates (for instance covering absence from work); and offering advice promotional to a healthy lifestyle. Some time will probably also be devoted to vaccination programmes or family planning.

GPs come into contact with all sorts of people, but the main medical conditions they deal with can vary greatly with the community, not least because psychological factors as much as physical ones can significantly affect health. For instance, where unemployment is widespread or physical work accounts for much of the employment available, rates of depression or industrial injury may be much higher than in a smart residential area. Similarly, a particular ethnic group may predominate, and the GP must be aware of any prevailing beliefs or practices likely to affect that community's health.

Despite recent reductions, GPs still work long hours, and much of their time is spent with people who are unwell. They therefore need to be physically fit, mentally alert, and emotionally resilient. They have to maintain accurate and informative records of all patient contacts, and keep up to date with new products and developments in treatment. Most surgeries include several doctors and time spent with colleagues is important for comparing information and professional experiences. Arrangements must be made to ensure that premises and medical equipment are in good order, that reception duties are clear and properly undertaken, and that any needed medical supplies are ordered in good time. The job therefore clearly has a business side to add to already considerable medical duties.

Some GPs are salaried, employed by PCTs, and earn between £52462 and £79167. Others are self-employed or part of a partnership holding a contract with a PCT, and typically earn between £80000 and £120000, depending on which services they offer and how they provide these.

HOSPITAL DOCTOR

Hospital doctors work mainly on wards or outpatient clinics. Some hospital jobs can be very hands on, as in, say, accident and emergency, or much more abstract or theoretical, such as laboratory work. The larger the hospital, the wider the range of roles likely to be available. Hospital doctors are more likely than GPs to work in teams and, for many, the day begins with a team meeting to discuss the patients to be seen that day. This is an excellent way to build up knowledge of a specialism, and to see how different colleagues and departments operate. Some aspects of hospital work may remind practitioners of life at the sharp end, especially in communities characterised by social friction, a drug or alcohol culture, or crime in general, things a suburban GP may encounter only occasionally or at least on a smaller scale. Hospital doctors are likely to work longer hours than GPs, and have to live in hospital when on call.

The pay of hospital doctors is a combination of their basic salary plus a supplement based on the number of hours over 40 which they do each week, also taking into account the intensity of the work itself. Most junior doctors are on a supplement of 50 per cent of basic salary, and on this basis the annual pay would be £32 793. The typical pay of a doctor in his or her second year would be £40 674. A hospital doctor training for a specialism after a few years' experience would be on between £43 464 and £68 343. Consultants earn between £73 403 and £173 638, depending on length of service and performance-related pay awards. With private work, some consultants earn in excess of £250 000.

Here are some of the major specialist roles to which a qualified hospital doctor can aspire.

ANAESTHETIST

The popular image of the anaesthetist is of someone who puts a patient to sleep and ensures unconsciousness throughout a major operation. Of course, this is part of their role, but their pre-operative work is also designed to ensure the patient is in the best condition possible to come through an operation, and emerges from it comfortably. Anaesthetists also play an important part in accident and emergency work, resuscitation, acute and chronic pain management, obstetrics, and transfer of patients from one hospital to another. Anaesthetics began to be used in the 1840s, and for many years entailed dangers of their own, despite the terrible suffering they avoided. Procedures are now very safe, however, with fewer than four deaths per million patients being directly anaesthetic-related. Anaesthetics is part of a broader field known as intensive care medicine (ICM). Training normally becomes available after a few years' general experience as a doctor, at the level of senior house officer or registrar, and includes assessment by examination. Further information is available from the Royal College of Anaesthetists (tel: 020 7092 1500; website: www.rcoa.ac.uk).

GERIATRICS

The term 'geriatric' derives from the Greek word *geron* meaning 'old man', and geriatric specialists deal with all medical conditions which particularly affect older people. The most pressing current issue in the field is delirium, the confusion and disorientation which can lead to other medical complications, thereby prolonging the patient's hospitalisation. Effectively countering this is done by keeping the patient stimulated and constantly oriented to reality. Another problem with older people, particularly those not in hospital but taking medication, is their difficulty in correctly administering this, owing to confusion or memory loss. One study has shown that a quarter of those asked about this admitted to taking incorrect dosage or skipping their medicine altogether. Doctors in this field concern themselves with the remedial and social elements as well as the clinical and preventative ones, so while well-acquainted with conditions commonly affecting the elderly, such as arthritis, osteoporosis, and Alzheimer's disease, they also must know how to combat dementia and depression. There is a specialism called psychogeriatrics, allowing doctors interested in this area to become particularly knowledgeable. Rehabilitation work is very important, too, often involving short-term intensive physical therapy in the aftermath of treatments such as joint replacement.

PAEDIATRICS

Paediatrics is a field dedicated to curing or minimising the effects of medical conditions in children (regarded in most cases as those aged up to the mid-teens or so). Increasingly, paediatricians treat many inherited diseases (such as cystic fibrosis) whose sufferers would not previously have lived into adulthood, and much of their focus is on congenital defects and features of development. A lot of training is needed to recognise in children the difference between normal variants in maturation, and what is pathological and deserving attention. Paediatrics also involves issues of legal jurisdiction. Because many children cannot make informed decisions for themselves, practitioners often deal with the parents and guardians of their patients. Professional training for paediatrics can begin after medical training plus some years of hospital-based experience. Further information is available from the Royal College of Paediatrics and Child Health (tel: 020 7307 5600; website: www.rcpch.ac.uk).

NEUROLOGY

The field of neurology is concerned with disorders of the nervous system, which is itself divided into three main parts – the central nervous system (brain and spinal cord), peripheral (the co-ordination of body movements) and autonomic (automatic processes such as heartbeat, breathing rate and digestion).

Practitioners diagnose and treat conditions and, because the field is one in which important advances have been made rapidly, clinical trials and other research are likely to constitute part of their remit. The range of conditions neurologists deal with include migraine, stroke, sleep disorders, cerebral palsy, brain tumours, Tourette syndrome, Alzheimer's disease, meningitis, coma, and speech and language disorders. Much of the initial work with patients is testing their strength, co-ordination, reflexes, and sensation, in an effort to make an initial diagnosis. Some treatments and monitoring can be left to the patient's GP, but more serious cases may be referred to a psychiatrist or even a neurosurgeon.

FASCINATING FACTS

The human brain weighs about 3lbs, and the cerebellum constitutes the largest and most important part of it. In 1824 a Frenchman named Flourens demonstrated that the cerebellum was the area responsible for acts of thought and will.

PATHOLOGY

Pathologists use a range of investigative techniques (including biopsies and autopsies) in order to detect disease, but mainly by examining organs, tissues, cells, and body fluids. This is often essential to a correct diagnosis which will ensure appropriate treatment. Detecting the source of a disease may also be essential to arresting its spread. Much of the work is laboratory-based, with electron microscopy and molecular biology playing important roles. Its effectiveness, however, depends on good links between those on the science side and those doing clinical work. Pathologists do not usually see patients, acting instead as sources of information for other doctors. They normally undertake about six years of training following their medical degree, but some workers in pathology laboratories hold a higher degree in a science subject (MSc or PhD) rather than a medical qualification. Further information can be obtained from the Royal College of Pathologists (tel: 020 7451 6700; website:www.rcpath.org).

PSYCHIATRY

Psychiatrists study, prevent and treat mental disorders, and (unlike most psychologists) are qualified doctors. During the twentieth

century, a biological basis for many mental conditions was
established, and it became necessary for practitioners to have
a foot in two camps – the social sciences and the biological ones.
Psychiatry has been described as a middle ground between
neurology and psychology, and deals with three main areas: mental
illness, personality disorder, and severe learning difficulties. Much
of the work is done in community settings as well as in hospitals,
and certain specialisms such as forensic psychiatry – assessing and
treating offenders with disorders – may be done in custodial ones.
Psychiatrists often therefore work with non-medical professionals,
such as teachers or social workers, as well as the families of their
patients. The scrutiny of certain conditions, together with the
importance of continuity in establishing patient–practitioner
relations, may mean working with some patients over a long
period. Further information is available from the Royal College of
Psychiatrists (tel: 020 7235 2351; website: www.rcpsych.ac.uk).

PALLIATIVE MEDICINE

The term 'palliative' derives from the Latin word *palliare*, meaning
to cloak, and palliative medicine is concerned with the physical and
mental relief of patients (including those who are dying) rather than
their cure. Once associated mainly with patients in the later stages
of cancer, it is an approach now increasingly used with those
suffering chronic heart failure or progressive neurological
conditions, and there are whole teams in hospitals whose work is
focused on palliative care. However, where hospices cater only for
those near the end of their lives, hospital-based care results in over
half of all patients improving sufficiently to return home (at least
temporarily). Patients are often fearful of the future, their loss of
independence, and being a burden to others as well as of pain and
perhaps aspects of their treatment. Practitioners must therefore
deal with major psychological effects as well as physical ones, and
may call in colleagues or non-medical professionals to assist in
certain cases.

SURGERY

A qualified doctor with a few years' experience can undertake basic
training in surgery, which takes two years. This allows him or her to
select an area for special training, of which there are nine: general;
orthopaedic (correcting deformities); neurological; paediatric
(surgical care of children); plastic (often for reconstructive work,

after burn injuries for example); cardiothoracic (dealing with the heart, lungs and oesophagus); ear, nose and throat; oral and maxillofacial (mouth, jaws, face and neck); and urinary (of the urinary tract). The training for any specialism is in the order of five to six years, and for the oral and maxillofacial specialism entrants have to be already qualified in dentistry as well as medicine. On successful completion of training, the surgeon can then apply for inclusion on the Specialist Register of the GMC, at consultant level. As well as undertaking operations, surgeons teach, deliver lectures, and carry out research. They may acquire new techniques and possibly can help develop these. Further information can be obtained from the Royal College of Surgeons of England (tel: 020 7405 3474: website: www.rcseng.ac.uk).

If you've not even begun basic medical training, these specialisms may seem hardly worth considering for at least a few more years. However, some investigation of them at an early stage may make a good impression on university selectors. If admitted to medical school, you may also find that a particular module or elective allows you to undertake project work which fires your ambition to enter a particular field, and there are other specialisms in addition to those mentioned here.

MATURE ENTRY

Most people who go to university do so straight after A levels at age 18, or 19 if they take a gap year. The obvious advantages of this are engaging in the whole higher education experience with people of your own age and obtaining a degree before making some of life's bigger commitments, such as a mortgage or a family. However, not everyone is sure of their career direction while still in their teens, and most medical qualifications are fairly job-specific. It's therefore hardly surprising that some people don't opt for a relevant course until into their 20s, or older still. If you do this, what are the prospects of getting a place?

During the past 10 years or so, an increasing proportion of successful applicants to medical school have been 21 years old or over, and now over 20 per cent of entrants fall into this category. Many begin conventional medical degrees, but some embark on four-year graduate entry programmes often known as the 'fast-track' route. About half of the 32 British medical schools offer these, most requiring a class 2:1 degree in a relevant subject, such as a biological science, for eligibility. The British Medical Association's (BMA) policy is to encourage applications from suitably qualified people regardless of age, and while its stance has contributed to a reduced resistance to mature applicants, some schools still favour younger ones. Anyone not eligible for a fast-track course may still attract selectors if offering significant experience of work in a health, caring, or relevant science field. Successful applicants with a degree in a non-science subject would be required to undertake a pre-medical year to gain the necessary science background.

APPLICANTS WITH DISABILITIES

The Disability Discrimination Act (1995) obliges universities to take into account the needs of students suffering from chronic illness or disability. Medical schools are not exempt from this regulation and good practice holds that the school should first assess the applicant on the same criteria as everyone else. Only after this should physical or other limitations be taken into account as a necessary aid to the selectors' decision. This calculation has to be made not only in the light of study demands, but also with an eye to those of the foundation programme spent in hospitals. Applicants should recognise that the level of support within institutions will vary, and speak to admissions staff well in advance, as well as reading available information. A medical career is demanding even for very capable and able-bodied people, and anyone with a disability, however enthusiastic and talented, should think carefully about whether they will be able to cope.

PORTRAIT: LOUIS PASTEUR (1822–1895)
Louis Pasteur was a French chemist and microbiologist best known for his breakthrough work on the causes and prevention of disease. Among his early significant research was his work relating to the fermentation process, notably of milk and wine. Pasteur's experiments demonstrated that this was caused by micro-organisms, and not the spontaneous generation which was still believed in some quarters. He, in turn, invented a heating

process which killed most of the moulds and bacteria which occurred, making these drinks much safer. This came to be called by a name it still bears today – pasteurisation. This led him to conclude that micro-organisms infected humans and animals, too, and his proposal that the entry of these into the human body should wherever possible be prevented was the trigger for Joseph Lister to develop antiseptic methods in surgery. Pasteur was not the first to put forward this 'germ theory', but his experiments were most effective in demonstrating its correctness, and convincing practitioners and those in authority across Europe that it was true.

Pasteur's work on diseases included studies on chicken cholera, which led him to produce an inoculation against anthrax, a disease known predominantly for its decimation of animal populations, mainly cattle. He also produced a treatment for rabies, which was first used on a nine-year-old boy who had been badly bitten by a rabid dog, and proved a spectacular success. Pasteur termed these treatments 'vaccines' in honour of Edward Jenner who had developed a treatment for smallpox through cowpox (*vacca* is the Latin for cow). The distinctive feature of Pasteur's vaccines was that they had been generated artificially, avoiding the need to find a weakened form of the disease in order to effect treatment.

Pasteur was one of the most eminent Frenchmen of his day. The Institut Pasteur, founded in his honour, has since 1908 produced eight Nobel Prize winners in the fields of medicine and physiology.

CHAPTER 5

Other medical professions and training

In a book of this size, it's not possible to offer a picture of every job in the medical spectrum. However, those featured here have been chosen because they are popular among people with ambitions to work in medicine and because they offer a sufficiently representative selection of the responsibilities, tasks, satisfactions, difficulties and career options in medicine for you to decide whether you want to find out more.

DENTIST

Dentists offer dental checks and treatments to patients, either through the NHS or privately. Many people have a check once or twice a year and, even if no remedial treatment is needed, have their teeth cleaned professionally or are offered advice about long-term care. Where required, treatment may take the form of a filling or extraction or (frequently for cosmetic reasons) the fitting of a bridge, brace, crown, or dentures. These last four require careful measurement, and an impression is usually taken to enable a dental technician to make the piece required. Dentists use sophisticated equipment, including adjustable patient chairs which enable them to work sitting down, much reducing the risk of the back strain once an occupational hazard. They work in sterile conditions, wearing surgical gloves, safety glasses and a protective coat or jacket, and provide patients with safety glasses for some jobs.

Most dentists work in a practice with at least one other dentist, and are supported by reception staff and at least one dental nurse or hygienist. Their working hours are more predictable than doctors': a typical week is 9am–5pm or 6pm, Monday to Friday, with the possibility of a Saturday morning or early evening opening on one weekday, plus an emergency service, usually shared with other local practices. Dentists working in the community see patients of all ages, from young children upwards, and must be able to reassure them, since many will be a little nervous even if not in pain. The work itself can be rather messy, and dentists must not be upset by the sight of blood. Manual dexterity and great care are also required. As well as their surgery work, dentists have to maintain patient records and liaise with colleagues and technicians who are probably based elsewhere. Some practitioners are employed in the hospital dental service, or the Armed Forces, and some by large companies which offer their employees in-house treatment. It's possible to specialise in a particular field of dentistry, such as orthodontics (rectifying crookedness in teeth), and some dentists also engage in research.

Dentists in community dental services are salaried by their Primary Case Trusts and earn between £36 000 and £78 000. Self-employed dentists who contract for NHS work earn between £60 000 and £120 000. The rates for consultants in dentistry are as for consultant doctors. A dental nurse would normally begin at Band 3 of the NHS pay scale (£14 437–£17 257), rising to Band 5 (£19 683–£25 424). Dental technicians normally begin at Band 5 and can rise to Band 6 (£23 458–£31 779) for an experienced practitioner, and to Band 7 (£28 313–£37 326) for an advanced one.

TRAINING AND QUALIFICATIONS

To practise as a dentist requires successful completion of a five-year degree course in dentistry, for which excellent GCSEs and A levels are needed. The A level subjects should include chemistry and biology. Only 13 British universities have a dental school.

Dental technicians normally require A*–C grades in at least four GCSE subjects, including English, Maths, and a science. A BTEC National Diploma in Dental Technology is offered at some colleges or dental hospitals, and Higher National Certificate and degree courses are also available. However, the National Diploma is sufficient for most posts, and some dentists may offer in-house training and day-release for this.

For dental nursing, A*–C grades in from two to four GCSE subjects are normally required, English and Biology being the preferred subjects. Entrants normally undertake in-house training towards the National Certificate in dental nursing.

DIETICIAN

Dieticians (sometimes called food advisers) advise people about healthy eating. This can involve assessing the needs of individuals who may require a specific diet on account of a medical condition, such as diabetes, or may entail offering more general advice to groups of people, such as pregnant women or even schoolchildren. Many dieticians work in hospitals, where they not only see patients, but also liaise with the catering department about the suitability of general menus as well as particular patients' needs. They also communicate with medical colleagues and may be involved in research, spending time in a laboratory. Community-based dieticians can work in patients' homes, doctors' surgeries or clinics, and in some places may have an information role, writing leaflets aimed at the public, or reports for other professionals. As a dietician, it's very important to deal respectfully and sympathetically with people, and resist what may be a strong temptation to preach your message if you're to motivate them to follow a healthy regime which entails a major change in their eating habits. Your contact with them may be fleeting, and you must briefly show them what to do in a way they can accept and follow for themselves, as many long-term medical conditions are partly owing to, or exacerbated by, poor diet.

FASCINATING FACTS

In times gone by, sailors on long voyages ate limes to stave off a disease called scurvy. The area of London where these were stored is still called Limehouse.

Dieticians typically work 9am–5pm, Monday to Friday. It's a rapidly growing profession, with most opportunities within the NHS, but others in government agencies, the catering, food and pharmaceutical industries, and major retailers in the supermarket division, usually in an advisory capacity. Specialist work is available in gastro-entorology, or working with particular groups or individuals, such as professional sports teams or elite athletes. If the idea of working abroad appeals to you, there are increasing opportunities with aid agencies in developing countries. Some dieticians are freelance.

Dieticians usually begin on Band 5 (£19683–£25424), rising to Band 6 (£23458–£31779) for a specialist role, and Band 7 (£28313–£37326) for an advanced one.

TRAINING AND QUALIFICATIONS

Dieticians must have a degree in dietetics or a related degree (such as biology or food science) followed by a two-year Postgraduate Diploma in Dietetics. Entry to either route requires at least five GCSEs at A*–C grades, plus A levels which include Chemistry and one other science subject. Most first-degree courses in dietetics last three years. A BTEC National Diploma in a relevant area may be an acceptable alternative to A levels.

Profile: Joan – Dietician

I'm a dietician working with mental health patients, and I specialise in eating disorders. With each patient, I first have to assess their food intake and eating behaviour generally then try to gauge the extent of their knowledge of nutrition, and how far they're motivated to change. In most cases I have to educate the patient about the business of nutrition, and do this with family members, too, as they're often a big factor in the success or otherwise of any programme I devise. Some patients aren't eating enough, and for them I usually prescribe multivitamin supplements as well as an appropriate menu. Most of my clients are anxious or depressed, and I let any other professionals dealing with them know about the dietary changes I've planned. In turn, they can often tell me things which might help me fine-tune these changes. You need to be a good listener to do this work, as it's not just about telling people what's good for them. You have to understand their fears, dislikes and preferences, and point of view before you can judge their real needs and come up with a programme which has a real chance of working. I don't use a lot of sophisticated equipment, but a weighing machine, calculator, skin callipers (to measure muscle and fat) and a tape measure are all essential. The biggest challenge in this job is to motivate people to eat things they're not used to, but which are vital for their health to improve. In the long term I may take training in psychotherapy, as this would help me address more of the issues in patients' lives which lead to their eating disorders.

OCCUPATIONAL THERAPIST

Occupational therapists (OTs) design programmes of activity to help people cope with problems (usually physical, but sometimes psychological or social) which have arisen on account of ageing, illness or injury. The goal may, for instance, be to get an elderly person moving easily around their home again, or help a relatively young and vigorous person return to work. A plan is produced by the OT which is tailored to the patient's current and potential capacity, the environment in which they will have to live or work, and takes account of all important factors, physical and otherwise, such as reduced confidence or motivation.

The success of a rehabilitation programme may depend heavily on modifications to the patient's living or work environment. The OT therefore needs to look at their home or workplace, and talk with them about what they do there, before any modifications are made or special equipment is introduced. Though not responsible for fitting adaptations, OTs need to know what devices are available, and which might suit the setting and the individual. They also need to instruct patients in using equipment, to let them do this confidently themselves. Getting patients to accomplish physical exercises, revive old interests or socialise, are all important contributions the OT can make to their recovery, but it is in showing them *how* to accomplish these, rather than just urging them to, that the OT's skill lies. Also, a surprising amount of helpful devices are available to patients free of charge from local clinics, and OTs can authorise the use of these for as long as they're needed.

As well as their patients, OTs will often find themselves speaking with relatives and employers, who need to understand the patient's requirements and limitations. Traditionally, OTs have long been part of the NHS, but increasing numbers now work in local authority social services departments. Like all health professionals, they meet with colleagues, and will discuss patients with social workers, too. A driving licence will probably be essential for the job.

Occupational therapists normally begin on Band 5 (£19 683–£25 424), rising to Band 6 (£23 458–£31 779) for specialised work, and Band 7 (£28 313–£37 326) for an advanced role.

TRAINING AND QUALIFICATIONS
OTs must have a degree in occupational therapy, for which five GCSE passes at A*–C grade, plus A levels, one of them preferably in Biology, are required. A relevant BTEC National Diploma may also be acceptable. Applicants holding a degree in a relevant subject (such as biology, psychology, or sociology) may also be accepted, but must complete the two-year Postgraduate Diploma in Occupational Therapy.

PHARMACIST

Most pharmacists are community-based, supplying treatments to the public in high-street pharmacies or the increasing number of pharmacy sections of large supermarkets. They make up prescriptions issued by doctors and advise customers on the use of medicines (including alerting them to possible side-effects). They can also provide information about healthy living generally, including how to deal with minor injuries and skin conditions, and how to give up smoking. They maintain detailed records, and may have a role supervising and training pharmacy technicians. Typical working hours are 35–40 a week, including one late evening and some weekend work, possibly on a rota basis. All pharmacy work requires great care and attention to detail, as mistakes may have very serious consequences.

Pharmacists working in hospitals are responsible for the ordering, storage and distribution of drugs and other medicines used there. They organise the delivery of these products to wards, and supply outpatients with their prescribed treatments, usually in the form of tablets, capsules, creams, liquids, or even injections. They also make up medicines in quantities sufficient to meet the demands of a large number of patients, including those being treated for cancer, sometimes with intravenous medications. They must manage a budget for all this, and keep individual wards informed of their own expenditure. They may run training sessions for clinical staff about drugs and their effects, particularly those newly on the market. They have contact with patients, some of whom will need instruction in how to take or apply their medication. Hospital pharmacists may work for the NHS or in the private care sector. Their hours are usually 9am–5pm, Monday to Friday, plus some evening and/or weekend work, usually on a rota basis.

Industrial pharmacists work in the pharmaceutical sector, developing, manufacturing, testing and marketing new drugs. They may specialise in fields such as clinical trials or even animal medicine.

NHS pharmacists usually start on Band 5 (£19 683–£25 424), progressing to Band 6 (£23 458–£31 779) as a matter of course. Assuming a higher responsibility, such as team leader, would merit Band 7 (£28 313–£37 326). Salaries for pharmacists in industry, with a drug Company, for example, can be much higher.

TRAINING AND QUALIFICATIONS

Qualified pharmacists have to complete a four-year degree course in pharmacy and a pre-registration year of salaried work experience before being admitted to the Royal Pharmaceutical Society of Great Britain. Entry to degree courses requires a good range of A*–C GCSE passes (preferably A*–Bs) and good grades at A level, including Chemistry and two other sciences.

RADIOGRAPHER

There are two kinds of radiography: diagnostic and therapeutic. Diagnostic radiographers normally work in a hospital or clinic. They use high-tech equipment to produce images of organs, bones and other bodily parts, and interpret the significance of these to help doctors diagnose and treat injuries or conditions. They often work in accident and emergency units, but can also work on wards using mobile equipment. Traditionally, radiographers have used X-rays, but now also employ techniques such as computed tomography (CT) scanning, magnetised resonance imaging (MRI) and ultrasound. Therapeutic radiographers normally work only in the radiography departments of large hospitals, delivering prescribed treatments, mostly for cancerous conditions. This entails setting up radiation equipment to an exact dosage for a precise time, to target affected tissue while minimising the effects on surrounding areas. All radiographers deal directly with patients, but therapeutic workers may get to know patients quite well, as many will have repeat treatments at intervals of only a few weeks. A sympathetic manner is important, as a proportion of patients are unlikely to recover, but enormous satisfaction can be gained by seeing the majority restored to partial or complete health. Radiographers need to have a considerable amount of anatomical knowledge, be able to cope with some unpleasant sights, and be fit and strong enough to lift or otherwise move patients into the position necessary for treatment.

Diagnostic and therapeutic radiographers usually begin on Band 5 (£19 683–£25 424) rising to Band 6 (£23 458–£31 779) for a specialist role, and Band 7 (£28 313–£37 326) for an advanced one.

TRAINING AND QUALIFICATIONS
Radiographers hold a degree in radiography, diagnostic radiography or therapeutic radiography. Many progress by then taking a Postgraduate Diploma in subjects such as CT Scanning or Medical Ultrasound. Entry to degree courses normally requires A*–C grades in at least five GCSE subjects, plus A levels which include at least one science subject, preferably Physics or Maths.

PHYSIOTHERAPIST

Physiotherapists use a number of techniques, including massage, electrical treatment and water therapy (or hydrotherapy) to help patients recover from disease or injury. They also assist elderly people and anyone recovering from the effects of an operation to regain some of their former movement, strength and flexibility. They teach their patients how to do remedial exercises unsupervised, and encourage them to overcome any barriers (whether physical, social, psychological, cultural, or environmental) to their recovery. Physiotherapists keep records of their patients, and discuss them with healthcare colleagues when necessary. Fitness and strength are needed to lift patients or manoeuvre them into position for treatment, and at least basic swimming skills are necessary for hydrotherapy. Most physiotherapists work within the NHS, but some are employed in private practice, sports clinics, health spas, and within business and voluntary organisations, as well as residential care organisations and patients' homes. Within the NHS, the working week is typically 9am–5pm, Monday to Friday, but in other organisations or private practice, some evening and/or weekend work is to be expected.

Physiotherapists within the NHS normally start at Band 5 (£19 683–£25 424), rising to Band 6 (£23 458–£31 779) for specialist work (in such fields as orthopaedics, obstetrics, sports therapy, or work with elderly people), with Band 7 (£28 313–£37 326) for an advanced role, which might include teaching, research, or management responsibilities.

TRAINING AND QUALIFICATIONS
Would-be physiotherapists take a degree course in physiotherapy, normally lasting three years. Entry is normally through A*–C grades in at least five GCSEs, with A levels which include Biology and/or Chemistry. The BTEC National Diploma in Health and Social care may be an acceptable alternative.

MEDICAL PHOTOGRAPHER/ ILLUSTRATOR

Medical photographers visually record operations and other medical procedures. This may be to facilitate the diagnosis of a condition, but is often for scientific or research purposes in medical journals or textbooks, or for educational materials, such as audio-visual teaching aids used in lectures or seminars aimed at a range of medical professionals. Sometimes very sophisticated methods or equipment (including ultra-violet or infra-red photography) are employed, for instance in taking pictures of internal parts of the body, and a number of sessions over a period may be needed to show the development of a condition or healing process, with careful shot selection and lighting to ensure that even quite subtle changes are apparent. Photographers need medical knowledge as well as photographic skills, and some specialise in forensic photography, working with a pathologist to produce results which may be used as evidence in court cases. This is definitely not an option if you're squeamish!

Medical illustrators use their artistic skills to produce complete or partial images of the human body and of medical conditions. Sometimes three-dimensional models are required, for which a fuller medical knowledge is needed than for most photographic projects. Some practitioners specialise in surgical illustration, medical animation, or facial reconstruction. Like photographers, illustrators typically work a 9am–5pm day, Monday to Friday, but may be on call outside these hours, especially for forensic work. Sometimes a photographer and illustrator will work together, especially in operating-theatre jobs. Freelance work is available in both specialisms.

About two-thirds of those doing this work are self-employed. Fully qualified practitioners working within the NHS would be likely to start on Band 6 (£23 458–£31 779) and could rise as high as Band 8B or C (£42 064–£52 002).

TRAINING AND QUALIFICATIONS
Entrants to this work normally already hold a degree in photography, graphic design, or illustration. Photography graduates can undertake a two-year in-service training, while those with other degrees take a year longer. Trainees normally obtain a Postgraduate Diploma/MSc/MPhil qualification in Medical Illustration or Medical Art. Entry to the first-degree courses mentioned normally requires some A*–C grades at GCSE, plus a BTEC National Diploma in an art/design subject. Applicants offering A levels including Art will also be considered, but are likely to have to complete a one-year Foundation course in Art/Design before starting their degree.

PARAMEDIC

Paramedics respond to 999 calls and give emergency treatment to victims of accidents or people suddenly taken ill. They operate mostly in conventional ambulances, but also motorcycles (which can get through traffic very quickly) and air ambulances to reach places which are otherwise inaccessible or unreachable speedily. Paramedics are highly trained and can employ advanced life-support equipment, administer drugs to stabilise a patient before transportation to hospital, or even use resuscitation techniques where the patient is unconscious or near death. They monitor patients on the way to hospital, keeping a close eye on vital signs such as breathing and blood pressure, and setting up an intravenous drip where necessary. Because their initial tasks are often undertaken at the scene of road accidents, paramedics work closely with the police and fire service. They may be on duty (according to shift) at any hour of the day or night, and must be physically fit and capable of heavy lifting. While most medical jobs entail a measure of unpleasantness, this can be particularly true for the paramedic, who may be first on the scene, and be presented with individuals who are unconscious, in severe pain, deep shock, or dead. Enormous satisfaction is to be gained from helping establish order in chaotic situations, and getting people to medical settings where they can begin their recovery. There will, of course, be many occasions where, despite every effort, the ending is less happy.

Paramedics start at Band 5 (£19 683–£25 424), rising to Band 6 (£23 458–£31 779), with the prospect of Band 7 (£28 313–£37 326) for a service area manager. In addition, paramedics are paid an allowance of up to 25 per cent of basic pay for unsocial hours and standby duties.

TRAINING AND QUALIFICATIONS

Entry requirements vary, but typically three to five GCSE passes at grades A*–C, to include English, Maths and a science are needed. It is possible to train first as an ambulance technician, and after 12 to 18 months' experience, apply for paramedic training, for which there is strong competition. The course lasts 10 weeks, six being classroom-based, and four in hospital departments. Direct entry is also possible through a degree course in paramedic science.

FASCINATING FACTS

Heart rate tends to vary with the size of the organism. Humans average about 72 beats a minute, with elephants about 20, and the shrew (the smallest mammal) about 1000!

OSTEOPATH

Osteopaths use manipulation to relieve pain and remove stiffness in muscles and joints, taking account of the causes of their patients' discomfort, as well as their symptoms, recognising that the former and the latter may be in different parts of the body. Most people consult them for problems relating to the back, neck, and limb joints, but they can also treat symptoms related to asthma, arthritis, migraine, and tension in general. Osteopaths normally take a complete medical and lifestyle history of each patient before attempting a diagnosis or beginning treatment. If necessary, this is supplemented by blood or urine tests, or even X-rays. Manipulative treatment may be followed by advice on diet, posture, or an exercise programme, in an effort to avoid recurrence. You must be fit, and have strong hands, as the work is strenuous. Some osteopaths choose to specialise, perhaps in sports-related injuries. Not all musculo-skeletal problems can be helped by osteopathy and, where practitioners see this is the case, they will normally refer the patient to their GP in the hope of relief through other methods. Though now well respected, osteopathy's roots rest in the field of alternative rather than conventional medicine.

Osteopaths are nearly all self-employed, and charge fees rather than earning a salary. These usually fall within the range of £25–£50 a session, depending on the location and the practitioner's level of experience. Earnings are commonly around £20 000–£35 000, with established and experienced osteopaths typically earning between £35 000 and £50 000. Some earn more than £50 000.

TRAINING AND QUALIFICATIONS

Intending osteopaths undertake a four-year degree course in osteopathy. A shorter postgraduate qualification is also available to graduates in a relevant medical or scientific subject. An even shorter training is open to qualified doctors and physiotherapists, and an MSc degree is also available in Sports Osteopathy. Entry to degree courses usually requires a range of good GCSE passes, plus A levels which include Chemistry and Biology. Details of the relatively few accredited courses are available from the General Osteopathic Council (www.osteopathy.org.uk).

FASCINATING FACTS

Height across a population is often regarded as a good indicator of its standard of living and general well-being. The country with the tallest average is Holland, with 6'1" for men, and over 5'5" for women. However, in impoverished Southern Sudan, the Dinka tribe's men average 6'3" and its women 5'11" (but this is only across a population of 1.5 million). Currently the world's tallest man is a Ukrainian, Leonid Stadnyk, who stands 8'5". His extraordinary stature is accounted for by a pituitary gland tumour causing excessive secretion of growth hormone resulting in the condition known as acromegalic gigantism.

DISPENSING OPTICIAN/ OPTOMETRIST/OPHTHALMOLOGIST

Dispensing opticians work from the optical prescriptions supplied by an optometrist or ophthalmologist for patients. They supply and fit optical aids that have been prescribed (usually spectacles or contact lenses), measuring and checking lenses using sophisticated equipment. They also advise patients on the suitability of particular aids, taking into account cosmetic elements such as colour and shape, as well as fit and safety. About two-thirds of the dispensing market is represented by just four major retailers, and this is where the majority of dispensing opticians work, though a good many are in smaller outlets usually away from town centres.

Optometrists often work in the same outlets as dispensing opticians. They are responsible for testing patients' eyes and making a precise assessment of any corrective devices. They consult with dispensing opticians and with ophthalmologists, who are qualified doctors who have undertaken further training in the workings and treatment of the eye. Ophthalmologists normally work in hospitals, usually having consultant status, and diagnose and treat diseases or injuries to the eye. They can do operations to remove cataracts, cure astigmatism, and near- or far-sightedness. Some ophthalmologists progress to become experts on particular eye conditions, such as diseases of the retina. Eye specialists usually work a 35–40-hour week, with the likelihood of weekend work in the dispensing (retail) role. You must have good colour vision.

Earnings in this field vary a good deal, as about two-thirds of dispensing opticians are in private practice, with only a few in hospital eye clinics. Someone with between two and five years' experience could expect to earn £25000 and upwards, with £40000 a realistic target with significant experience. Most optometrists are also in private practice, but for those employed within the NHS, the range can be as wide as Band 5 (£19683–£25424) to Band 8D (£60669–£75114). Ophthalmologists are specialist doctors whose earnings would probably be in the range of £40000–£73000 until they acquire consultant status. Once achieved, their earnings are likely to be in the range of £73000–£150000-plus.

TRAINING AND QUALIFICATIONS

It is possible to take a diploma or a degree in ophthalmic dispensing. Five A*–C grades at GCSE, including English, Maths and science, would normally be required, plus one A level for the diploma route, two (minimum) for the degree, preferably to include a science subject. The BTEC National Diploma in Health and Social Care may be acceptable. Intending optometrists take a degree in optometry, ophthalmic optics or vision science, and often a postgraduate qualification for a specialism. The BTEC route may be possible, but usually applicants offer A levels which include at least two sciences. Ophthalmologists are qualified doctors who undertake additional training for this specialism (see above).

NURSE

Nurses are normally based in hospitals, clinics, local health centres, or residential care establishments. However, many have a role in the community, and visit patients in their own homes. Intensive and cancer care, as well as looking after elderly people, are among their major roles. All of these would be the province of someone in adult nursing, one of four available specialisms. Children's nursing is one of the others, and can range from the intensive care of a baby to helping teenagers injured in sports accidents. Learning disability nurses work to improve the health and independence of people who are unable to grasp everyday concepts or translate these into constructive action, and may spend most of their time in residential accommodation or private homes. Because about one person in every six suffers a mental illness at some time in their lives, mental health nursing is the fourth option, and in this field much more of the work than previously is done within the community. Nurses have a broad range of duties, which can be expected to vary considerably depending on the patient, the setting, and the circumstances. However, they can be broadly categorised as:

● assessing the physical, emotional, and social needs of patients and those close to them

● making arrangements for these needs to be met, often through the engagement of other professionals

● the control of physical pain or other discomfort through medication or therapy and

● the planning of care and rehabilitation programmes, often including an encouragement to self-help.

Specialisation after qualification is possible in many areas – from drug and alcohol abuse to theatre nursing – some specialisms require sustained contact with patients over long periods, while others are much shorter and intensive, as in accident and emergency.

A qualified nurse in the NHS would normally start at Band 5 (£19 683–£25 424), rising to Band 6 (£23 458–£31 779) for a specialist or team leader. A nurse team manager would be on Band 7 (£28 313–£37 326), and a nurse consultant on Band 8 ranges A–C (£36 112–£62 402).

TRAINING AND QUALIFICATIONS
There are two routes into nursing – the degree and the diploma. Both last three years, and entrants must normally be at least 17.5 years old. Five GCSE passes at grades A*–C, plus either A levels or BTEC National Diploma are needed for the degree route, but A*–C in GCSEs which include English and Biology may be enough for the diploma.

Profile: Christina – Senior Staff Nurse

I'm a senior staff nurse working on a surgical ward. We prepare patients for operations and take care of them immediately afterwards. There are 30 beds on the ward, and things get pretty busy at times. I do three (sometimes four) shifts of 12 hours every week, which can involve night duty as well as daytime work. I help to organise the work of staff for a given day, and make sure everyone knows what they're doing. I also go on ward rounds with doctors, and attend any meetings I need to. Through the day I spend time washing patients, helping serve meals, giving medications, and re-dressing wounds. I see relatives as well as patients, as a lot of people's recuperation takes place at home, so other people need to know what their limitations will be, so that they can help. Being part of a multi-disciplinary team, I speak with specialists such as physiotherapists, pharmacists and occupational therapists. We get quite a few students on the wards, too, and I act as a mentor to them. Every so often all the ward staff sit down and evaluate what we've been doing over a period of time, to see whether we should make changes, or request extra resources. In this job you need to enjoy working with people, and know how to communicate well with all sorts. It's also vital to be able to keep calm in emergencies, and to be ready to learn new things. I'm happy in what I do at the moment, and get enormous satisfaction seeing patients get well again, but in the long term I'd like to get promotion into a specialised nursing role, possibly in theatre work.

MIDWIFE

Unlike most of their medical colleagues, midwives deal with people who are healthy, but simply require assistance through a demanding but natural process. The midwife's task is to help pregnant women prepare for and manage the process of birth, and first contact with a mother-to-be is usually two to three months into her pregnancy, then every month or so until the last four to six weeks, when weekly visits are likely. Though only a small proportion of births give rise to complications, most women, their partners and families benefit from support during the pregnancy through detailed advice and information on a range of matters, from ante-natal clinics to feeding, or just from the reassurance that an expert is keeping an eye on things. Women giving birth in hospital have a medical team to hand in the event of difficulties, but if any occur during a home birth, the midwife can call in a doctor for assistance. A good proportion of midwives enter the profession after having trained and worked as nurses, and an abbreviated training is open to those who wish to take that route. Experienced midwives can progress into family planning, training, and management. Training in midwifery is open to both males and females.

Entry pay level for midwives is normally Band 5 (£19 683–£25 424) rising to Band 6 (£23 458–£31 779). A team manager could expect to be on Band 7 (£28 313–£37 326), a consultant midwife on Band 8 ranges A–C (£36 112–£62 402).

TRAINING AND QUALIFICATIONS

As with nursing, it's possible to train through the degree or diploma routes, with the same entry conditions applying. However, qualified nurses can obtain a midwifery qualification through a shortened (18-month) training programme. Similarly, a graduate with a relevant degree (for example, human biology, physiology or other medical specialism) can become qualified via a slightly longer (two-year) programme.

ENVIRONMENTAL HEALTH OFFICER

Sometimes also known as public health officers, environmental health officers (EHOs) are employed to ensure healthy living and working conditions for people. This is achieved sometimes through preventative work, such as checking the outbreak or spread of disease. The job entails a lot of inspection work, for example of the storing and handling of food in shops, restaurants and canteens, food processing plants, and even abattoirs. This can involve operating specialised equipment capable of delivering precise readings, used not only in commercial or industrial premises, but also to ensure houses are fit for habitation, and that levels of noise and pollution don't exceed legal limits. The job is office-based, but most of the work involves visiting people and places and frequently calling on legislation to enforce decisions, to the extent of making court appearances, normally in the service of the prosecution. A more agreeable part of the job may be giving advice; a less agreeable one is making unpopular decisions which result in a fine or, in more serious cases, the closure of a business. Inspection work may take place in surroundings which are dusty or otherwise unpleasant, and for which protective clothing must be worn. Most EHOs work for local authorities, but some are employed in the private sector by hotel and catering establishments, while others find places in the NHS, Armed Services, or even within the holiday industry, checking hotel accommodation for tour operators. The office part of the job entails writing very detailed and accurate reports, which may form the basis for legal action. There is strong competition for training as an EHO, and relevant work experience or some work shadowing is important prior to application, along with formal education requirements.

Salaries for this work vary with the employer, but generally fall within the range of £25 000–£35 000. With experience this can rise to between £35 000 and £60 000, and a director of public health could expect to earn about £70 000.

TRAINING AND QUALIFICATIONS

To become an environmental health officer it is usual to take a degree in environmental health or environmental science, which normally last three years. Entry requirements to first-degree courses normally specify a minimum of five GCSEs at grades A*–C, plus two or three A levels, one of which is in a science subject. Another route into the work is through a science degree followed by a two-year MSc degree in Environmental Health.

SPEECH AND LANGUAGE THERAPIST

Speech and language therapists help people to overcome physical or psychological obstacles to communicating comfortably and effectively. Therapists may work with people who are the victims of accidents or degenerative conditions, but also those whose difficulties arise from a traumatic experience or other emotional blockage. One fairly common psychologically-based problem reducible or even curable through therapy is stammering. Therapy itself may involve patients learning muscle control, or the therapist introducing a technical device which amplifies or clarifies the patient's voice. Treatment may be necessary over a long period, and the therapist must have the patient's trust from the outset. Sessions are usually on a one-to-one basis, but group work can sometimes be a good way to encourage and motivate individuals who may otherwise feel isolated. Most speech and language therapists are based in a hospital or clinic, but many also visit patients in their homes, too, where they may also show family members how they can support the patient, perhaps by helping them complete prescribed exercises. Most therapists work a conventional Monday to Friday week, but some evening or weekend work is possible, especially for those in private practice.

A newly qualified speech and language therapist within the NHS would start on Band 5 (£19 683–£25 424), and an experienced specialist would be on Band 6 (£23 458–£31 779). An advanced therapist would be on Band 7 (£28 313–£37 326), and a principal or consultant therapist on Band 8 ranges A–C (£36 112–£62 402).

TRAINING AND QUALIFICATIONS
The route into this work is a degree course in speech and language therapy, speech sciences or human communication. Grades A*–C in at least five GCSEs, plus A levels/BTEC National Diploma are normally required. Preferred or required A levels may include Biology and/or a modern language. Graduates whose degree is in a subject such as psychology, linguistics, or biological sciences may be considered for a postgraduate qualification shorter than the three-year degree course.

CHIROPODIST/PODIATRIST

Chiropodists (also called podiatrists) diagnose and treat injuries and other conditions of the foot and lower leg. These include dealing with corns, hardened skin, skin infections, and problems arising from inactivity, poor posture, or walking technique. Chiropodists perform minor surgery, but also encourage their patients to improve by giving them foot exercise programmes, and play an important role in helping older people to remain independent by getting about comfortably. They employ drugs and chemicals, apply dressings, and use smaller pieces of equipment such as a scalpel or small drill (for nail work). Sophisticated techniques such as ultrasound and hydrotherapy are also part of their armoury, as well as massage, and appliances like special insoles which they can fit into patients' footwear. Because a proportion of their patients are likely to be immobile, some home visits are likely to be part of their duties, but most chiropodists work in a hospital, clinic, or health centre. The typical working week is 35–37 hours, Monday to Friday, but private work may entail some weekend and/or evening activity. Quite a lot of chiropodists combine NHS and private work, and some receive patients in their own homes. Specialist work in biomechanics may be an option for the experienced practitioner.

Most podiatrists are employed by the NHS once qualified, and can expect to earn from Band 5 (£19 683–£25 424) through Band 7 (£28 313–£37 326). Senior podiatrists/chiropractors, who often combine NHS work with private patients, usually earn between £35 000 and £50 000.

TRAINING AND QUALIFICATIONS
A degree course in chiropody/podiatry is the normal route into the work, with A*–C grades in at least five GCSEs, plus A levels being the stepping-stones to this. One or two science subjects may be required at A level. Applicants with a relevant degree (such as physiotherapy, biology, or nursing) may be granted exemption from part of the course.

MEDICAL LABORATORY ASSISTANT

Medical laboratory assistants support the activities of professionals such as biomedical scientists and technicians, and are usually employed in a hospital or possibly a research unit or institution. Much of their work is in specialised fields – such as pathology, haematology or immunology – and usually involves setting up tests and recording and analysing the resulting data using computers, labelling samples and disposing of chemical waste. Lab workers are usually on their feet a lot of the time, and need to maintain high levels of care and concentration. They work with medical laboratory scientific officers (usually under their supervision), but are unlikely to meet patients. They're responsible for checking stock levels and ordering fresh materials as required.

Medical laboratory assistants in the NHS are usually employed on Band 1 (£12 182–£13 253) or Band 2 (£12 577–£15 523). Some who specialise in areas such as phlebotomy (testing blood) or cytology (testing for abnormal cells), earn more, normally Band 3 (£14 437–£17 257).

TRAINING AND QUALIFICATIONS

It is often possible to begin work as a medical laboratory assistant with A*–C grades in three to five GCSEs (preferably including English, Maths, and science), and gain the necessary knowledge largely through on-the-job training. Posts for laboratory technician often require A levels/BTEC National Diploma in a science or health-related subject, and sometimes even a specific degree (for example, biomedical sciences).

PROSTHETIST/ORTHOTIST

Prosthetists design and fit artificial replacements for limbs or other body parts. Mostly this is for patients who have lost (or been born without) one or more arms or legs. The work entails taking careful measurements and a plaster cast of the area onto which the replacement is to fit, and then to make a prosthetic limb (using a variety of materials, including plastic, leather, metal, and carbon fibre) which is safe and comfortable, as well as fully functional. Orthotists do slightly different work, providing surgical appliances such as splints, collars, and braces for people with problems of posture or movement. For instance, an orthotist might make special shoes for a patient with an arthritic condition. Prosthetists and orthotists need to be good communicators as well as technically expert, as they must find out the exact nature of the patient's needs and limitations. Often a number of adjustments to an aid or replacement are needed before the patient feels happy with it, and only then can the practitioner begin to instruct them in how to use it. Most of the work with patients is in hospitals and clinics, but some involves visits to the places where the prostheses (artificial replacements) and orthoses (surgical appliances) are made.

There are no nationally-agreed pay rates for these jobs, but a new entrant would be likely to earn between £20000 and £25000, rising to £30000–£35000 with experience. Senior prosthetists/orthotists can earn £50000-plus.

TRAINING AND QUALIFICATIONS

A four-year degree course in prosthetics and orthotics is a requirement to do this work. Applicants normally hold a minimum of 5 A*–C GCSE passes, plus A levels which include two science subjects. Those offering BTEC National Diploma in a relevant subject may be considered if it has been awarded with distinction.

HEALTH SERVICE MANAGER

Health service managers are responsible for commissioning and delivering health care in a given locality, normally through hospitals, community health centres, and general practice surgeries. General managers deal with several main areas, including budgets, welfare, staffing allocation, and information. In very large hospitals, however, a manager is more likely to have a specialist function, such as strategy planning, personnel, or security. Much of the work entails meetings with colleagues or representatives of other organisations, analysing information, writing reports, giving presentations, liaising regularly with particular departments and doing general paperwork. In some exercises, staff opinion needs to be gauged in advance of a decision, which may bring the manager into contact with colleagues at all levels. Ability to interpret statistics and to think on your feet can be especially useful skills in the job. Moving into management may be possible for a medical practitioner, particularly if their role hitherto has involved responsibilities such as supervising and training staff, and adhering to a budget, rather than patient care exclusively. Most management jobs are within the NHS, but opportunities also exist in the private sector and the Armed Forces.

Someone starting with the NHS as a manager could expect to be on Band 6 (£23458–£31779) if responsible for a section within a department such as catering or finance. A team leader within such a department would normally be on Band 7 (£28313–£37326), while a departmental head would be somewhere in Band 8 (£36112–£75114) depending on responsibilities, the size of the department, and the nature of the work.

TRAINING AND QUALIFICATIONS

Entrants to the work are normally graduates, some of whom hold a relevant degree, such as in health service management, public administration, or business management. However, a specific degree is not essential, and the NHS offers a graduate training scheme open to applicants holding at least a class 2:2 degree in any discipline. As with most other degree courses, five A*–C grades at GCSE, plus A levels/BTEC National Diploma (or equivalent) is the entry route.

CREATIVE THERAPIST

Creative therapists work with people who have trouble expressing themselves, or who need stimulation to encourage them to engage in activities. Often, their patients have long-term learning difficulties, but others may need help following a traumatic experience. Practitioners need considerable sensitivity to build up each patient's trust sufficiently for them to co-operate in addressing their problems. They must establish an environment which the patients find unthreatening and non-judgemental and in which they can explore their feelings or beliefs free of censure or ridicule. This may be achieved on a one-to-one basis, but therapists often work with groups, when encouragement and sense of well-being can be obtained through shared experiences and achievements.

There are six specialisms within creative therapy: art, music, drama, dance, horticulture and play. Creative therapists can work in varied settings – including hospitals, clinics, special schools and prisons – as well as in private practice, and liaise with medical professionals (including clinical psychologists), non-medical professionals (for example teachers, youth and social workers), and with family members. There are relatively few opportunities for creative therapists, and some begin on a part-time basis, perhaps combining this with some other form of health or caring work. Most therapists work a Monday to Friday week, but some evening and/or weekend work may be necessary or desirable, especially in private practice.

Of creative therapists, those specialising in art, music and drama are probably the best-paid, with earnings of between £20 000 and

£30 000 in the early years, £30 000–£45 000 with experience, and
£50 000–£73 000 for someone reaching consultant level. Play,
drama and horticulture therapists would be likely to remain within
the range £20 000–£35 000.

TRAINING AND QUALIFICATIONS

Art, music and drama therapists come under the jurisdiction of the
Health Professions Council, and only those registered with it after
completing approved training can work within the NHS. Entrants
normally hold a degree in the relevant area (art, music, or drama),
and follow this with a Postgraduate Diploma course over one or two
years. Dance, horticulture and play therapists, though not under the
Health Professions Council, take qualifications through their
professional body, delivered by or at a university. Most are
graduates.

Profile: Geoff – Music Therapist

I'm employed within the community music therapy service
and try to help people suffering from a range of conditions,
which include autism, dementia and depression. Normally I
see each of my clients once a week for half-an-hour, and
during a typical day I see five or six. We create music
together, working in a large room which contains a good
range of instruments, though for some people, singing is a
better option. What we actually do depends on the aim of the
session, but some people find music a good alternative to
speaking, while others find it a good memory-trigger, and it
boosts nearly everyone's confidence. Sessions can be quite
intensive, and my contact time is comparatively short because
I need time to record in detail what's been accomplished with
each person, for which I have a separate office. I'm also out
and about a good deal, going into clients' homes, hospitals,
hospices and care homes, when I take with me just a small
selection of portable instruments. In this job, whatever your
preferred instrument, it helps to be able to play the piano to
at least intermediate level. In some sessions we just listen to
music, and sometimes I compose a short piece to achieve

something very specific. However, I must emphasize that this job is not about teaching people how to play or sing, but how to use music in helpful ways. Although most of my work is with individuals, some of the most pleasurable sessions I've done have been with groups, when the enjoyment can be really infectious.

CLINICAL PSYCHOLOGIST

Clinical psychologists work with patients who are mentally ill, depressed, or have severe learning difficulties, anxieties, obsessions, addictions, or other behavioural or social problems as a result of poor health. In fact, it's not uncommon for a patient's problem to be the result of a physical condition (such as disablement or HIV/AIDS) severe enough to unbalance them emotionally and psychologically. The clinical psychologist assesses the patient through observation, tests and interviews, to determine the nature of his or her problem and determine the best method for tackling it, which may include counselling or some form of therapy. The psychologist will liaise with fellow professionals, both medical and otherwise, so a social worker could be included along with an occupational therapist. Psychologists are also keen to involve members of the patient's family, something especially important when dealing with one who is uncooperative or aggressive. When not in direct contact with patients and workplace colleagues, clinical psychologists are busy writing reports and patient notes, keeping their knowledge up to date, and attending training and conference events.

Clinical psychologists' earnings usually begin at between £20 000 and £25 000, and can easily rise to £40 000–£45 000 with experience. Very experienced psychologists with responsibilities for managing staff can earn in excess of £60 000.

TRAINING AND QUALIFICATIONS

A three-year degree course in psychology is required, with a minimum of five A*–C grades in GCSE subjects, plus A levels. Interestingly, A level Psychology is not normally required, though many entrants to degree courses will have developed their interest partly through the A level course. It is important that the psychology degree course you take is one relevant to the work and approved by the British Psychological Society (BPS), as this is essential for admission to the necessary postgraduate training.

BIOMEDICAL SCIENTIST

Biomedical scientists carry out a wide range of laboratory tests on medical specimens, such as blood samples, tissue and body fluids, to help doctors diagnose conditions and monitor and treat their patients. Most are based in hospitals, and serve all departments, often doing tests for diseases such as cancer, HIV/AIDS, anaemia and diabetes, as well as taking samples at operations or post-mortems. They employ very sophisticated equipment, including electron microscopes, and keep meticulous records of what they do. They need to be observant, patient, accurate, analytical, able to work unsupervised, not be squeamish and wear protective clothing. This is an all-graduate profession, and all degree courses must be approved by the Institute of Biomedical Science. Some courses incorporate the necessary in-service experience. Besides NHS posts, there are opportunities in government departments, private hospitals, pharmaceutical firms, laboratories, universities and research institutes. Once qualified, most biomedical scientists specialise in a particular area, such as clinical chemistry, haematology (study of the blood), cytology (study of plant and animal cells), virology (study of viruses), medical microbiology or immunology. A typical working week is 37 hours and those based in hospitals are likely to work shifts, which will include nights if the hospital offers 24-hour service.

Biomedical scientists working in the NHS normally start at Band 5 (£19 683–£25 424), progressing through Bands 6 and 7 with experience (£23 458–£37 326). A few may earn more than this.

TRAINING AND QUALIFICATIONS
Entrants normally hold a degree in biomedical sciences or biological sciences. The prerequisites for this are normally at least five A*–C GCSEs, plus A levels which include Biology and Chemistry. Postgraduate training courses of one or two years are also open to graduates in a relevant (that is medical-related or scientific)

discipline. Many biomedical scientists go on to take a doctoral degree (PhD) in a very specialised field of Investigation.

CHIROPRACTOR

Chiropractors diagnose and treat problems of the musculo-skeletal system by hand manipulation, mainly of the spinal region. Much of their work is to give their patients relief from stress or poor posture, to offset the effects of lack of exercise, or as part of the rehabilitation process following an accident or illness. The practitioner first takes the patient's medical history, does a physical examination, and may carry out tests if there's any doubt as to whether chiropractic treatment is appropriate. In addition to manipulation, treatment may include advice on diet or exercise, and possibly a specific programme on one or both of these. A single treatment may be enough, but more often patients return for follow-up manipulations and checks on progress. There are over 2000 chiropractors in Britain registered with the General Chiropractic Council.

Normally self-employed or part of a partnership, chiropractors earn fees per session, typically at rates between £30 and £60 per treatment. Initially, earnings would probably be in the region of £20 000–£30 000, with experienced practitioners typically earning £40 000–£50 000. Very experienced and able practitioners may earn in excess of £80 000.

TRAINING AND QUALIFICATIONS
Would-be chiropractors take a degree course in chiropractic, which is offered at only three approved training institutions in Britain – in Bournemouth, Oxfordshire and South Wales. Courses last four or five years, and A levels which include two sciences are likely to be required.

FASCINATING FACTS

There are 206 bones in the adult human skeleton, including 27 in each hand, 26 in each foot, and 22 in the skull. Newborn babies have over 300 bones, but many of these knit together later.

COMPLEMENTARY MEDICINE PRACTITIONER

Acupuncture, Alexander technique, aromatherapy, herbal medicine, homeopathy, hypnotherapy, naturopathy, and reflexology are among the best-known specialisms open to anyone interested in complementary medicine. They are alike in focusing on the whole person, taking account of lifestyle, emotional and spiritual health, diet and environment as well as bodily condition, an approach known as 'holistic'. While some work within the NHS, the majority of the 50 000 complementary practitioners in Britain operate from home, in a health spa, or complementary health centre.

Acupuncture is an ancient Chinese technique (but one recognised by the WHO) which involves inserting fine needles at precise points of the body to relieve pain, anaesthetise (for example for operations) and treat a wide range of conditions, including asthma, high blood pressure, arthritis, migraine, and addictions. The British Acupuncture Council says that training should last a minimum of three years, and a few degree courses are available.

The **Alexander technique** shows patients how to become more aware of their own bodies in everyday life, and to reduce or eliminate bad habits which cause strain or other problems, with a view to improving stance, movement, and weight support. No formal qualifications are needed to begin training, but anyone interested is advised to visit a course provider to obtain a basic knowledge of the technique before applying.

Aromatherapy employs essences distilled from plans and mixed with oil to alleviate stress and other conditions. Practitioners take a detailed patient history and then apply the appropriate oils by massage.

Homeopathy is based on the natural tendency of the human body to heal itself, and practitioners prescribe their patients minute doses of substances which would produce symptoms of the condition in a healthy person. Some homeopaths work within the NHS.

Naturopathy avoids the use of drugs or surgery, but includes techniques such as dietetics, manipulation, exercise, hypnotherapy, relaxation, counselling, and positive thinking to promote and maintain the body's self-healing mechanisms.

Reflexology entails applying pressure to specific points in the hands and feet, to release blockages in the body's energy pathway, which reflexologists believe is essential to good health.

Hypnotism is used to relieve a wide range of physical, psychological and emotional conditions, and many professionals working in conventional medicine have taken training to add this to their skills armoury.

Finally, **herbalism** (a very ancient practice) uses remedies which combine natural plant sources with oil to treat illness and correct perceived imbalances in the body. Herbalists diagnose problems and offer holistic treatment, which includes advice on topics such as diet and lifestyle, as well as supplying herbal prescriptions.

Such is the range of therapies, their relative popularity and the ambitions of practitioners, that there are wide differences in earnings among complementary therapists. The majority probably earn between £20000 and £50000, if working full-time.

TRAINING AND QUALIFICATIONS

Training and qualifications are much less standardised than within the NHS, and some specialisms have more than one professional body. However, all have codes of conduct, training and operational standards which must be complied with. Many entrants to complementary medicine have experience within the caring, grooming, or conventional health professions. Full-time courses are the norm for some specialisms, but training by part-time or even distance learning is possible in others.

PORTRAIT: WILLIAM ROENTGEN (1845–1923)

William Roentgen was a German physicist who, at the University of Wurzburg in 1895, was investigating external effects from vacuum tank equipment when he noticed that invisible cathode rays caused a fluorescent effect on a small coated cardboard screen. In the course of testing out this effect on a different tube with a thicker glass wall, he noticed a shimmering effect on a laboratory bench some distance away. Considering that a new kind of ray might be the cause, Roentgen threw himself into investigation, eating and sleeping in his laboratory. A few weeks after first noting the phenomenon, he took the first X-ray picture, of his wife's hand. While later exploring the capacity of a range of materials to block the rays, Roentgen saw the first radiographic image, his own flickering skeleton on the screen, and later reported deciding at that point to continue his experiments in secret, lest his professional reputation suffer if his observations were wrong.

Roentgen wrote his first academic paper about his discovery and had it published before the end of 1895. It was titled 'On a new kind of rays', and was followed by two more over the next two years. His discovery would have guaranteed a considerable income but it did not make him wealthy because he refused to take out the patents on his invention. His work was recognised, however, and earned him the first Nobel Prize awarded for Physics, in 1901. Roentgen died at the age of 77, of cancer, though the cause of his death was not believed to be connected with his investigations, as he was one of the few pioneers in this field who employed protective lead shields. He is the father of diagnostic radiography.

CHAPTER 6

Preparation and application

Considerable preparation is advisable before attempting to enter any career, but this is especially true for medical work, because of the high commitment required. The work will make demands on your organisational skills, knowledge, intelligence, care and efficiency, as well as your ability to deal competently and compassionately with patients who may have very different needs. Also, because considerable training precedes entry to almost any job in the medical field, study must be undertaken and high-level qualifications obtained before you can begin to practise. This is true whether you hope to become a doctor, nurse, pharmacist, paramedic or radiographer, or one of the many other jobs on offer. You can't just pick it up as you go along!

IS MEDICAL WORK RIGHT FOR ME?

There are two main ways to assess whether a medical career is worth aiming at, and it's important to do both. One is to make an informed and honest judgement of the kind of person you are, and match your aptitudes and inclinations with the nature and requirements of medical jobs in general. You could begin to do this by seeing how far you already meet the personal qualities outlined in Chapter 3, and thinking carefully about any over which you have doubts. Because the range of medical jobs is so wide, it may be that a quality essential for one role is less vital for another.

The second way is to compare your academic interests and abilities with the entry requirements for training. For many (though not all) of the jobs featured in Chapter 5, an appropriate degree is required, with good GCSE and A level/BTEC results (often in specific subjects) the route to this. However strong your enthusiasm, or even your personal qualities, no hospital or university will admit you to a training course unless convinced you can cope with the study. If you are weak in any required subjects, you'll have to decide whether it's worth the effort of trying to make improvements to the extent you'd need to.

There are some things worth saying in connection with self-assessment. Firstly, it's often hard to trust our judgement of ourselves, so you may find it useful to ask a few people whom you know and trust whether they think you have the qualities already identified as important. You can feel reassured if they think you do, but any doubts they express should give you pause for thought. However, people can be mistaken, and a more objective method would be to use a career match computer program, such as KUDOS. This offers you job suggestions based on your answers to a series of questions about your likes and dislikes, strengths and weaknesses. The program will no doubt highlight more than one career worth your attention, but if medical work is not among them, it's unlikely that you'd be suited to it. You should also ask yourself for how long you're willing to study, since progress to a higher level is rarely (if ever) possible without the appropriate professional qualification. Nursing is one job for which two entry routes are available – degree or Diploma – but even the Diploma (though not normally requiring A levels/BTEC) still takes three years.

Once you've thought all this through, you should arrange to have a talk with a careers adviser, either in your school or college, or at your local Connexions centre. The adviser will discuss your ideas with you, and alert you to anything of particular importance and tell you what your next steps should be. Any doubts which the careers adviser expresses about your suitability for a career in medicine should be taken very seriously.

FINDING INFORMATION

A number of reliable resources are to be recommended to help you build up your knowledge. A good one to start with is the NHS website (www.stepintothenhs.nhs.uk), which features material on dozens of interesting areas of medical work, as well as items about current medical issues, events, and information about pay and training. If you know what medical work you'd like to do, an excellent link is the professional body representing those working in that specialism, and contact details for many of these are given in Appendix 1. The website above is usually sufficient for most people's needs, but you can telephone or email most professional bodies if you have a specific enquiry. Other good sources are your school or college library (there's often one devoted solely to careers), and the one at your local Connexions centre. Care is taken in all of these to ensure that material is current, but be careful about buying careers books in shops or borrowing them from public libraries, as these are not always up-to-date. As a general guideline, read with caution any occupational material more than two years old, and do ensure that any decisions or choices you make are based on accurate information.

Whatever medical specialism you may be considering, you should be aware of general issues to do with health, a few examples of which have been given in Chapter 2. News broadcasts and documentaries can, over time, provide you with a good background, and make it easier for you to stay up-to-date. This is especially important if you aspire to a job whose role is wide-ranging, such as a doctor or nurse. Would-be doctors, in particular, should consider taking a good newspaper on the day it has a medical feature, as this is where prominent issues are debated by specialist correspondents or distinguished practitioners, and where technical aspects are described as well as social implications taken into account. Chapter 7 also features a list of books and journal publications covering the range of medical specialisms described in Chapters 4 and 5.

WHAT'S IT REALLY LIKE?

As well as reading, and discussing your plans with people, it's essential to do some work experience or work shadowing. Without this, however reliable your resources, your picture of a medical environment will be at best limited and could at worst be seriously mistaken. The best place in which to undertake work experience/shadowing is probably a hospital, but a local health centre or GP surgery may provide a good alternative. A single, intensive week may be most convenient for you, but a day or evening once a week over a period may enable you to learn more or get to know in more detail how things are done. Either way, helping, observing and asking questions (without being a nuisance) should prove very valuable. If you can't go to a hospital, you may like to approach a local hospice, which cares for terminally ill people. Most hospices welcome volunteers since, as charitable organisations, they have smaller budgets than NHS hospitals. The nature of their work may make your time there emotionally demanding, but also be a good test of your resolution and capacity to cope with the less pleasant features of medical work. Work shadowing is more likely to be a single visit than an ongoing commitment, allowing you to focus on one practitioner. Prepare and ask good questions which invite the person you're watching to draw on his or her experience to answer. Remember, though, that an effective medical service depends on co-ordination and teamwork as much as the skills of individuals, and talk to staff who, though rarely in the limelight, contribute significantly to patients' treatment and recovery, even if indirectly. They include technicians, healthcare assistants and administrators. While on work experience or shadowing, keep a diary; this obliges you to think about your impressions at the time, and is likely to prove very valuable when making an application or during an interview.

POST-16 OPTIONS

If you've not yet taken your GCSEs, work hard to get the best grades you can, particularly in English and a science subject. It's very unlikely that you'll be offered training for any job with medical responsibilities unless you hold at least grade C in five subjects, including these two. Entry to any medical training usually requires you to be at least 17, so would-be entrants spend one or (more often) two years obtaining the next level of academic or relevant vocational qualification, usually A or AS levels, or a BTEC First or National Diploma. The most relevant A or AS levels for medical work are Chemistry and Biology, with health and social care or early years/childcare good options within the BTEC range. If your school has a sixth form, get a copy of its prospectus, and find out the date of its next open evening. Have a look at what's on offer at other local sixth forms and colleges, too. Be prepared to change school/college in order to start the course most suited to your ambitions. If you'd prefer to gain relevant experience which is workplace-based, and study for a relevant qualification at the same time, then consider an apprenticeship in health and social care or early years care. However, be warned – this route is suitable for entry to only a limited range of medical jobs, most notably nursing. You can apply, if you wish, for both apprenticeships and for full-time courses until you see what offers you get, or reach a decision on your long-term plans.

RESEARCHING COURSES

There are well over 100 universities in Britain, and many of them offer medical courses of one sort or another. Taking time to find a course you feel will be right for you personally, as well as appropriate to your career plans, is just as important as the decision of which career to follow. Look closely at the prospectus and/or website of a number of institutions, paying particular attention to how the relevant courses are taught and examined, and to any options within them which might appeal to you. Wherever possible, go to an open day to see what the university looks like, and to get a sense of what it might be like to study there. Remember that you may not be offered a place at the university you'd most like to attend, so you must look at a few others just as seriously.

MAKING APPLICATIONS

Most applications to university are made between 1 September and 15 January of the academic year preceding entry to the degree course. These are made through UCAS, the central admissions body and (except for medicine, dentistry and veterinary science) can be made to up to five institutions. Almost without exception, applications are made electronically, and your school or college will tell you how to do this. The electronic method allows you to fine tune your application without wasting paper, and for it to be processed much more quickly than in the past. You should take considerable trouble over your personal statement, whatever your intended course, as this is where you effectively argue your case for consideration. It's probably best to split this into clear subdivisions or paragraphs, ordering and linking these coherently. Keep sentences brief but informative, and above all, grammatical. Say enough to gain the reader's interest, but don't go into too much detail, as this can be done at an interview. Take care not to miss out anything important, such as a work experience, the reason for a special interest, or a science project you've done which relates to medicine. Ensure that at least one suitably-qualified person (such as your head of sixth form, college personal tutor, or careers adviser) reads it through, and take seriously any comments made, especially changes suggested, and if in doubt, get a second opinion. Don't try to complete your application in one go; come back to it, several times if necessary, and fresh each time. This will allow you to see it as would someone reading it for the first time, and therefore to be constructively critical. Don't come to regret not having made the effort which might have earned you a place.

PREPARING FOR INTERVIEWS

It's unlikely you'll be offered a place on a medical training course without being interviewed, so you should take this part of the procedure as seriously as any other. There are two main things to consider in advance – self-presentation (what to wear, how to sit, how to speak etc.), and the questions you might be asked. Regarding dress, you should err at least on the smart side of casualness, and an unashamed attempt at smartness (for example a suit) might be safer, and certainly won't lose you marks. It may ease nerves to rehearse (and on the day adopt) a sitting posture which is comfortable, respectful, and doesn't suggest stark terror! Try to speak in a calm and measured way, even if this is slower than usual, and take a moment to consider a question if you need to – the panel won't run away. Some schools and colleges offer students mock interviews to iron out self-presentation glitches and get them used to talking about themselves. This can be hard to do with people you know, but may lead to excellent advice which boosts your chances. Also, because some institutions coach their students into polished performers, you may be disadvantaged if you arrive at the real thing completely cold. The strength of competition for places on courses means that you should do in advance everything which you think might help you appear at your best when it really matters.

FOR DOCTORS AND DENTISTS ONLY

It's important to draw attention here to a few significant differences between applicants for courses in medicine and dentistry, and the rest. Anyone wishing to be considered for either of these two specialisms must submit their UCAS form by 15 October, three months earlier than the deadline for other undergraduate courses, and only four of the five course options may be used for medicine or dentistry (leading many applicants to leave the last slot blank, or choose a medical-related or other science subject). The early deadline means that it's very much in your interests to have completed all your course research, work experience or shadowing and university visits by the September of the year you apply (for most candidates, the start of Year 13), leaving only the form itself to be done by mid-October. The intense competition for places on these courses has led a large proportion of medical and dental schools to introduce computer-based aptitude tests as an additional means of assessing applicants. The best-known are the UK Clinical Aptitude Test (UKCAT) and the Biomedical Admissions Test (BMAT). The former is the more widely used, but both are taken in the autumn preceding entry, around the time you make your application through UCAS. The tests assess verbal, quantitative and abstract reasoning, and decision-making. Competition has encouraged some would-be doctors and dentists to seek their training abroad. In some countries, there are medical and dental degree courses offered in English; see Chapter 7 for more details. There are complications in taking this route, but if you're very determined, have strong personal qualities and a big sense of adventure, you may want to find out more. *Very* early research on this is advisable.

THE PREPARATION TIMETABLE

At the beginning of A levels or a BTEC National Diploma, university application can seem a long way off. However, after allowing for adjustment to your new study format, revision and exam periods, and around 13 weeks of holidays, what looks like a year can quickly shrink to half that time. A part-time job may further reduce the time you can devote to career investigation, and you should take care not to do paid work for more than 8–10 hours a week, or your academic performance is likely to suffer, too. All things considered, you really can't afford to begin the process of reading, work experience and career-testing much later than January of the year you apply, particularly as when you can speak to practitioners or spend time in a hospital or other medical facility will depend on when people there can fit you in. Get your teachers on your side by telling them your career plans; this will encourage them to get the best out of you, and alert you early on if your work slips below target grades. As well as their emotional support, parents or other relatives can play an important practical role, too, for instance by driving you to a university open day. However, be considerate – don't just tell them you'd like a 200-mile lift the night before!

APPLYING FOR MEDICAL JOBS

If and when you begin training, you'll soon become aware of where medical jobs are advertised, and how to enquire about opportunities in particular places. This is because information about jobs will be made available within the university or hospital where you train. Another excellent source is the website of the appropriate medical professional body. This should be especially useful if you want or need to move to find work, rather than being committed to just one area. However, if your focus is geographically confined, it's worth trawling through local newspapers, especially in the months approaching course completion, which is likely to be the early summer. If you have an enjoyable work placement in the course of training, you might enquire about the possibility of a job there when you've qualified, as you may have already earned favourable consideration. You'll also see medical jobs advertised in the journal of the relevant professional body, and in national newspapers, perhaps in the form of a regular feature or supplement. Some medical specialisms offer only few opportunities for newly qualified people, and enquiries about these should be made very early. For certain kinds of post, a part-time appointment may be the only kind available, but this should soon provide enough experience to allow you to apply for full-time posts with more confidence. The application procedure itself is now increasingly done online.

FASCINATING FACTS

A pioneer of the modern microscope was the Dutchman Anton Van Leeuwenhoek, some of whose lenses could magnify up to 200 times. In 1676 he detected what modern science now refers to as bacteria.

PORTRAIT: ALEXANDER FLEMING (1881–1955)

Alexander Fleming was a Scottish biologist and pharmacologist who is famous for the part he played in the discovery and development of penicillin, the first antibiotic. Fleming served as a captain in the Army Medical Corps and, while in France during the First World War, saw many soldiers die of infected wounds. At that time the conventional wisdom was to treat these with antiseptics; however, although these worked well near the surface, they actually sheltered harmful bacteria further in, and it was these which led to so many deaths. After the war, Fleming returned to St Mary's Hospital, in London, where, in 1923, he became Professor of Bacteriology.

Though a doctor and a scientist, Fleming had a reputation for not being the tidiest of workers, and his laboratory contained many neglected items. Late in 1928, he returned from a long holiday to find a number of the cultures he had left there contaminated with a fungus. Ordinarily he would have discarded these unexamined, but on inspecting them, found on one a fungus on which bacteria could not grow. He checked its anti-bacterial effect on numerous organisms, and among those it affected were scarlet fever, meningitis, pneumonia and diphtheria, all very serious and often fatal conditions at that time. Fleming published his findings in the *British Journal of Experimental Pathology*, but it attracted little attention, and many of the tests made on penicillin proved inconclusive. Fleming himself recognised the difficulties of producing it in the necessary quantities, and, feeling it had little future as a treatment, abandoned his research on it in 1940.

However, the Second World War being by now under way, scientists at Oxford University named Florey and Chain, with funding from the British and American governments, did the research which made mass production of penicillin a viable proposition, and it appeared on the market soon afterwards. In the year 2000, less than 60 years after it was first used, it was estimated that penicillin had saved around 200 million lives. Fleming died in 1955; his laboratory at St Mary's Hospital is now home to the Fleming Museum.

CHAPTER 7

Finding out more

A book of this size and fairly general scope can offer no more than an introduction to the field of medicine and some of the better-known jobs within it. It has served its purpose if you feel it has told you enough to say that you're not after all attracted to a medically related career, or if it's raised your interest sufficiently to want to know more. If you *are* interested, this chapter offers suggestions of how to obtain the additional knowledge about medical careers and about yourself to decide whether to try to train for a particular job.

BOOKS, JOURNALS AND WEBSITES

Many people are attracted to a career in medicine, but find the sheer range of opportunities bewildering. This is where comparing jobs can be a useful way of teasing out the particular features which appeal to you. In this context, it's worth consulting the NHS careers website, as its abundant information on jobs and job categories make it easier to narrow down the options. You may soon reach a point where you focus only on jobs within one or two categories, and are able to reduce these as your knowledge and self-awareness grow, especially through work experience. The process of arriving at just one or two jobs that you're really serious about is likely to take

weeks or months, but examining general sources is a good way to
start.

Books and websites contain large quantities of information, and you
shouldn't waste time on material which isn't helping you progress.
Rather than try to read books or websites through, look at the
contents (or home) page, to see which chapters or sections might
interest you. Early on in your researches, only one chapter or
section may be worth your attention; as things progress, you'll
probably find yourself reading more, but within a narrower scope.

It's important to read material pitched at the right level. At the
beginning, publications aimed at practitioners will probably have
you scratching your head, and it's better to start with general
careers material until you have a reasonable grounding in a job
or medical field. In due course, you'll probably be able to extract
valuable information even from specialist material.

A list of further reading is given later in this chapter. Books on
medical topics can be quite expensive, and it's advisable to look
first in the careers library of your school or college, or your local
Connexions centre. There are plenty of good books available, but
buying any is probably better postponed until you're close to making
a firm career choice. Certain books and journals are obtainable
from specialist libraries through your local one (possibly for a small
charge) and from professional bodies (also listed below). Local
practitioners or medical centres may be willing to let you borrow
back numbers of professional journals.

TELEVISION AND RADIO

News programmes often run items on medical issues, but
frequently their angle is political or financial rather than health-
related, or they are featured because the circumstances are very
unusual. Perhaps a better way of gaining understanding of prevalent
medical matters is through good TV documentaries. The BBC's
Panorama and Channel 4 documentaries, in particular, often focus
on these from the perspective of patients and practitioners, and are
especially informative when they constitute a small series, as they
sometimes do. Weekly radio regulars such as *Case Notes* and *All in*

the Mind, hosted by an experienced doctor and psychiatrist respectively, feature guest consultants eminent in their field, while the contributions of patients and those close to them show how conditions can affect lives in ways likely to be illuminating. Supplementary material on appropriate websites is usually offered at the end of programmes.

OPEN/FAMILIARISATION DAYS

All universities hold open days when potential students can visit to look around, and during which most departments put on events or exhibitions designed to stimulate interest. However, the sheer popularity of such events may make it difficult to talk to medical school staff or students on the day. Some medical schools run intensive open days when you can attend lectures, take part in discussions and watch demonstrations, and some even offer summer schools, where you can stay on campus for two days or more, engaging in well-thought-out awareness-raising exercises, perhaps alongside current students. Some of these events are offered free, or at a nominal cost; others are run commercially, but include advice on the application process as well as insight into medical study and work.

TALKS, FEATURES AND MUSEUMS

It's not uncommon for a university to offer talks or lectures on medical topics, sometimes in the form of a series aimed at the intelligent layperson. These are usually delivered by a practising expert, such as a consultant, and can provide an excellent introduction to the issues and complexities which form an important part of certain topics or specialisms within health provision. Entry to such events is usually free or very cheap. You may also find it worth visiting a medical museum. London has several of these, while the Thackray Museum in Leeds focuses on the development of medicine during the past two or three centuries. It has exhibitions which explain bodily workings and medical techniques, instruments used in days gone by, and factors which played a significant part in the nation's health, including how the ignorance of doctors as well as patients contributed to the mortality rate. Visits to places like this can help to make medicine come alive by reminding us how far it has developed in a relatively short time, and perhaps inspire those with the commitment and ability to take it further.

BECOME AN 'EXPERT'

If (and only if) a particular medical field or topic interests you very much, you could set out to become an expert at it. Clearly you can't expect to become as knowledgeable as a practitioner, much less a consultant, but you could still realistically set out to obtain a good understanding. Provided you choose carefully so as not to make the focus too wide, this needn't entail endless hours of research; two or three general books on the topic, plus perhaps a dozen well-chosen professional journal articles consumed with a real effort to understand, should provide you with a body of knowledge impressive for someone not yet at the training stage. Such an exercise would have a twofold benefit by showing you what getting to grips with a medical topic is like, and furnishing an inviting feature for the personal statement of your UCAS application. Of course, this makes it likely that you'll be quizzed on it at an interview, but the alternative may be to be asked about something about which you know much less.

QUESTIONS TO ASK YOURSELF

It's easy to assume that everything you need to know about trying for a career in medicine is out there. In fact, every bit as important as knowing about qualifications, training, work experience, and medical specialisms, are a few things about yourself. Here are some questions to test your interest and motivation. It's worth putting them to yourself now, as you may even be asked one or two of them at a selection interview.

- Do I have enthusiasm and energy for most tasks I have to do?

- Am I sociable enough to enjoy working with a wide range of people?

- Can I work carefully and accurately?

- Am I fairly organised, and able to work to a programme or routine?

- Do I accomplish most practical tasks efficiently and tidily?

- Could I cope with the stress and strains of medical work, such as long hours or emotionally demanding cases?

- Could I stand the sight of blood, or of unhealthy bodies or unsightly conditions?

- Can I accept the restrictions which medical work might place on my private life and relaxation activities?

- Do I keep fairly calm in difficult situations?

- Am I keen to learn, and go on learning?

PORTRAIT: CHRISTIAAN BARNARD (1922–2001)

Christiaan Barnard first came to public attention in South Africa in 1959, where, six years after it had been done in the United States, he became the first surgeon there to perform a kidney transplant operation. For several years after this he experimented with animal heart transplants. The results were discouraging, but a number of breakthroughs were made in transplant surgery during the 1960s, and in 1967, in an operation lasting nine hours, and involving a team of 30, Barnard inserted a donated heart into Louis Washkansky, a 55-year old grocer suffering from diabetes and an incurable heart condition. Mr Washkansky lived only another 18 days, however, succumbing to pneumonia induced by the drugs used to suppress his immune system to encourage his body to accept the new heart. However, only two years later, Dorothy Fisher received a heart transplant from Barnard, and lived another 24 years, becoming his longest-surviving patient. Christiaan Barnard was photogenic, and became known as 'the film-star surgeon'. Hundreds of his patients were treated free of charge, and he used his fame to be an outspoken opponent of South Africa's discriminatory apartheid regime.

FURTHER READING

Books and Publications

A Career in Art Therapy?, British Association of Art Therapists
A Career in Speech and Language Therapy, Royal College of Speech
    and Language Therapists
A Guide to Careers in Environmental Health, Chartered Institute of
    Environmental Health
Becoming a Doctor, British Medical Association
Becoming a Psychologist, British Psychological Society
Careers in Chiropody/Podiatry, Society of Chiropodists and
    Podiatrists
Careers in Medical Illustration, Institute of Medical Illustrators
Getting into Dental School, Trotman
Nursing and Midwifery Uncovered, Trotman
So You Want to be a GP?, Royal College of General Practitioners
Study in Europe: Learn in English, Volume 1: Medical Sciences,
    Careerscope
The Biomedical Scientist, Institute of Biomedical Science
The Essential Guide to Becoming a Doctor, BMJ Books
The Work of Registered Dieticians, British Dietetic Association
Working in Complementary Therapy, VTCM/Connexions
Your Future in Pharmacy, Royal Pharmaceutical Society of Great
    Britain

Journals

Ambulance Magazine, Ambulance Service Association
BAPO Mag, British Association of Prosthetists and Orthotists (3
    times a year)
Blink, Association of Optometrists (monthly)
British Journal of Clinical Psychology, BPS (quarterly)
British Journal of Music Therapy, BSMT/APMT
British Journal of Occupational Therapy, College of Occupational
    Therapists (monthly)
Dietetics Today, British Dietetic Association (monthly)
Dramatherapy, British Association of Dramatherapists (quarterly)
Health Service Journal, Tower Publishing (weekly)
Osteopathy Today, British Osteopathy Association (monthly)
Physiotherapy Journal, Elsevier (quarterly)
Radiography, Society of Radiographers (quarterly)
Students BMJ (British Medical Journal), BMJ Publishing Group
The Lancet, Elsevier Ltd (weekly)

APPENDIX 1

Professional bodies

Professional bodies usually provide careers information on their websites, or in the form of a pack, for which there may be a charge. They are a good source of details of any changes in training or opportunity structures and of useful contacts or events in your area.

British Association of Prosthetists and Orthotists
Sir James Clark Building
Abbey Mill Business Centre
Paisley PA1 1TJ
Tel: 0141 561 7217
Web: www.bapo.com

British Chiropractic Association
59 Castle Street
Reading RG1 7SN
Tel: 0118 950 5950
Web: www.chiropractic-uk.co.uk

British College of Osteopathic Medicine
120–122 Finchley Road
London NW3 5HR
Tel: 020 7435 6464
Web: www.bcom.ac.uk

British Dental Association
64 Wimpole Street
London W1G 8YS
Tel: 020 7935 0875
Web: www.bda.org.uk

British Dietetic Association
5th Floor
Charles House
148–149 Great Charles Street
Queensway
Birmingham B3 3HT
Tel: 0121 200 8080
Web: www.bda.uk.com

British Institute of Professional Photography
Fox Talbot House
Amwell End
Ware SG12 9HN
Tel: 01920 464011
Web: www.bipp.com

British Medical Association
BMA House
Tavistock Square
London WC1H 9JP
Tel: 020 7387 4499
Web: www.bma.org.uk

British Paramedic Association
28 Wilfred Street
Derby DE23 8GF
Tel: 01332 746 356
Web: www.britishparamedic.org

British Psychological Society
St Andrews House
48 Princess Road East
Leicester LE1 7RD
Tel: 0116 254 9568
Web: www.bps.org.uk

Chartered Institute of Environmental Health
Chadwick Court
15 Hatfields
London SE1 8DJ
Tel: 020 7928 6006
Web: www.cieh.org

Chartered Society of Physiotherapy
14 Bedford Row
London WC1R 4ED
Tel: 020 7306 6666
Web: www.csp.org.uk

College of Occupational Therapists
106–114 Borough Hill Street
London SE1 1LB
Tel: 020 7357 6480
Web: www.cot.org.uk

Federation of Ophthalmic and Dispensing Opticians
199 Gloucester Terrace
London W2 6LD
Tel: 020 7298 5151
Web: www.fodo.com

Institute for Complementary Medicine
PO Box 194
London SE16 7QZ
Tel: 020 7237 5165
Web: www.i-c-m.co.uk

Institute of Biomedical Science
12 Coldbath Square
London EC1R 5HL
Tel: 020 7713 0214
Web: www.ibms.org

Institute of Healthcare Management
18–21 Morley Street
London SE1 7QZ
Tel: 020 7620 1030
Web: www.ihm.org.uk

Institute of Medical Illustrators
29 Arboretum Street
Nottingham NG1 4JA
Web: www.imi.org.uk

Royal College of Midwives
15 Mansfield Street
London W1G 9NH
Tel: 020 7312 3535
Web: www.rcm.org.uk

Royal College of Nursing
20 Cavendish Square
London W1G 0RN
Tel: 020 7409 3333
Web: www.rcn.org.uk

Royal College of Ophthalmologists
17 Cornwall Terrace
London NW1 4QW
Tel: 020 7935 0702
Web: www.rcophth.ac.uk

Royal College of Speech and Language Therapists
2 White Hart Yard
London SE1 1NX
Tel: 020 7378 1200
Web: www.rcslt.org

Royal Pharmaceutical Society of Great Britain
1 Lambeth High Street
London SE1 7JN
Tel: 020 7735 9141
Web: www.rpsgb.org.uk

Society of Chiropodists and Podiatrists
1 Fellmonger's Path
Tower Bridge Road
London SE1 3LY
Tel: 020 7234 8620
Web: www.feetforlife.org

Society of Radiographers
207 Providence Square
Mill Street
London SE1 2EW
Tel: 020 7740 7200
Web: www.sor.org

NHS pay rates under 'Agenda for Change' from 1 November 2007

Band number	Pay rates
1	£12 182–£13 253
2	£12 577–£15 523
3	£14 437–£17 257
4	£16 853–£20 261
5	£19 683–£25 424
6	£23 458–£31 779
7	£28 313–£37 326
8 Range A	£36 112–£43 335
8 Range B	£42 064–£52 002
8 Range C	£50 616–£62 402
8 Range D	£60 669–£75 114
9	£71 646–£90 607